AUSTIN TEXAS
Travel Guide
2024

Your Companion Guidebook To Exploring Nature, Culture, Must-See Attractions and Experiences for a Memorable Stay in Austin Texas.

Gregory X. Branham

1

TABLE OF CONTENT

Introduction to Austin

Overview of Austin's History and Culture

A Brief History of Austin

Austin's history traces back to the 1830s when settlers arrived in the area, initially known as Waterloo. In 1839, the city was officially named Austin after Stephen F. Austin, known as the "Father of Texas" for his role in the Texas Revolution and his efforts in establishing the Republic of Texas. The city quickly grew as a political, educational, and cultural hub.

One of the pivotal moments in Austin's history was the establishment of the University of Texas at Austin in 1883. The university has since become a cornerstone of the city's identity, contributing significantly to its intellectual and artistic vibrancy.

During the 20th century, Austin experienced economic growth driven by industries such as technology, music, and film. The emergence of the tech industry, with companies like Dell and IBM establishing a presence, earned Austin the nickname "Silicon Hills." The city's thriving music scene, highlighted by events like South by Southwest (SXSW) and Austin City Limits Music Festival, further cemented its reputation as a cultural hotspot.

Cultural Diversity and Influences

Austin's culture is a melting pot of influences, shaped by its diverse population and rich heritage. The city embraces a laid-back and creative lifestyle, attracting artists, musicians, and innovators from around the world. This cultural tapestry is reflected in Austin's vibrant arts scene, eclectic culinary offerings, and diverse neighborhoods.

One of the defining aspects of Austin's culture is its deep connection to music. From iconic music venues like the Continental Club and Antone's to the legendary Sixth Street, known for its live music performances, Austin pulsates with musical energy. Visitors can explore a wide range of genres, from blues and country to indie rock and electronic music, making it a paradise for music enthusiasts.

Austin's culinary scene is equally impressive, blending traditional Texas flavors with international influences. Food trucks, a ubiquitous sight across the city, offer a taste of local favorites like barbecue brisket, Tex-Mex tacos, and gourmet burgers. Additionally, Austin boasts a thriving craft beer and cocktail culture, with numerous breweries, distilleries, and speakeasies to explore.

The city's commitment to sustainability and outdoor living is evident in its abundance of parks, green spaces, and outdoor activities. Barton Springs Pool, located within Zilker Park, is a popular spot for swimming and picnicking, while Lady Bird Lake offers opportunities for kayaking, paddleboarding, and scenic hikes along the Ann and Roy Butler Hike-and-Bike Trail.

Preserving Austin's Heritage

Despite its modern development, Austin takes pride in preserving its historical landmarks and cultural heritage. The Texas State Capitol, a magnificent example of 19th-century architecture, stands as a symbol of Texas history and government. Visitors can take guided tours to explore its impressive interiors and learn about the state's legislative process.

For a deeper dive into Austin's past, the Bullock Texas State History Museum offers engaging exhibits on Texas history, including Native American heritage, pioneer life, and the state's role in the Civil War and beyond. The museum's interactive displays and artifacts provide a fascinating journey through time.

Key facts about Austin

Location and Climate
Austin is located in central Texas, bordered by the Hill Country to the west and the Colorado River to the south. The city enjoys a temperate climate with hot summers and mild winters, making it a year-round destination for outdoor activities and cultural events.

Population and Diversity
As of 2024, Austin is one of the fastest-growing cities in the United States, with a diverse population that reflects its vibrant culture. The city's residents, known as Austinites, come from various backgrounds, contributing to Austin's rich cultural tapestry.

Music Capital of the World
Austin is renowned as the "Live Music Capital of the World," boasting a thriving music scene that encompasses genres ranging from blues and country to rock, hip-hop, and indie music. Visitors can experience live performances at iconic venues like the Continental Club, Antone's Nightclub, and the Mohawk.

Technology Hub and Innovation
Beyond its music legacy, Austin is a major hub for technology and innovation, earning the nickname "Silicon Hills." The city is home to numerous tech companies, startups, and incubators, fostering a culture of creativity and entrepreneurship.

Cultural Landmarks
Austin's cultural landscape is dotted with significant landmarks and attractions. The Texas State Capitol, a stunning example of Renaissance Revival architecture, offers guided tours highlighting the state's history and government. The Blanton Museum of Art showcases a diverse collection of visual arts, while the Bullock Texas

State History Museum provides insights into Texas's past through interactive exhibits.

Outdoor Recreation
Nature enthusiasts will find plenty to explore in Austin's outdoor spaces. Lady Bird Lake, a reservoir along the Colorado River, is ideal for kayaking, paddleboarding, and hiking along the scenic Ann and Roy Butler Hike-and-Bike Trail. Zilker Park, home to the iconic Barton Springs Pool, offers picnicking areas, botanical gardens, and outdoor concerts.

Culinary Delights
Austin's culinary scene is a fusion of traditional Texas flavors and innovative dining experiences. From food trucks serving mouthwatering tacos and barbecue joints with tender brisket to upscale restaurants showcasing farm-to-table cuisine and international fare, Austin delights food lovers with its diverse gastronomic offerings.

Festivals and Events
Throughout the year, Austin hosts an array of festivals and events that celebrate music, culture, food, and creativity. South by Southwest (SXSW), a renowned gathering of film, music, and interactive media, draws international attendees. Other notable events include Austin City Limits Music Festival, Austin Food + Wine Festival, and the Trail of Lights during the holiday season.

University and Education
Austin is home to the University of Texas at Austin, a prestigious institution known for its academic excellence and research contributions. The university's campus adds vibrancy to the city, with cultural events, sports games, and educational opportunities for visitors and residents alike.

Transportation and Accessibility
Getting around Austin is convenient, thanks to a well-connected transportation system that includes buses, ride-sharing services, biking lanes, and pedestrian-friendly areas. The Austin-Bergstrom International Airport provides air travel options for visitors arriving from domestic and international locations.

Best times to visit Austin

Choosing the right time to visit Austin can significantly enhance your experience. Here are some key factors to consider when planning your trip:

Weather
Austin experiences a subtropical climate with hot summers and mild winters, making it a year-round destination. However, the weather can vary significantly throughout the year:

Spring (March to May): Spring is one of the best times to visit Austin. The weather is pleasant, with blooming wildflowers adding charm to the cityscape. It's ideal for outdoor activities like hiking, biking, and exploring parks.

Summer (June to August): Summers in Austin can be hot and humid, with temperatures often reaching the 90s°F (30s°C) or higher. While it's a popular time for festivals and outdoor events, be prepared for intense heat and occasional thunderstorms.

Fall (September to November): Fall brings cooler temperatures and less humidity, making it another excellent time to visit. You can enjoy outdoor activities comfortably and experience cultural events like Austin City Limits Music Festival.

Winter (December to February): Winters in Austin are mild compared to northern regions, but temperatures can still drop to the 40s°F (4-9°C). It's a quieter time for tourism, ideal for exploring indoor attractions and enjoying holiday festivities.

Events and Festivals

Austin hosts numerous events and festivals throughout the year, adding excitement and cultural richness to your visit. Some notable events include:

SXSW (South by Southwest): A renowned festival featuring film, interactive media, and music, usually held in March.

Austin City Limits Music Festival (ACL): A multi-genre music festival taking place in October, showcasing top artists from around the world.

Austin Food + Wine Festival: Celebrating culinary excellence with tastings, demonstrations, and food-related activities, typically held in April.

Formula 1 United States Grand Prix: A thrilling motorsport event held in November at the Circuit of The Americas.

Tourist Season

The peak tourist season in Austin coincides with events like SXSW and ACL, attracting visitors from across the globe. If you prefer a quieter experience with fewer crowds, consider visiting during shoulder seasons like late spring or early fall.

Outdoor Activities

Austin's outdoor attractions, including Lady Bird Lake, Barton Springs Pool, and Zilker Park, are best enjoyed during mild weather conditions. Plan your visit during spring or fall for comfortable outdoor exploration and recreational activities.

Accommodation and Prices

Hotel rates and accommodation availability can vary based on the season. Booking in advance, especially during major events, ensures you secure your preferred lodging at competitive prices.

Chapter 1:

Planning Your Trip

How to Get to Austin

Flying to Austin
Austin-Bergstrom International Airport (AUS) serves as the primary gateway to the city, located about 5 miles southeast of downtown Austin. It's a modern and efficient airport with multiple domestic and international flights. Here are some key points regarding air travel to Austin:

Domestic Flights: Major airlines like American Airlines, Delta Air Lines, United Airlines, Southwest Airlines, and JetBlue Airways operate frequent flights to Austin from various cities across the United States.

International Flights: While Austin-Bergstrom International Airport mainly caters to domestic flights, there are select international routes, especially to nearby destinations in Mexico and the Caribbean.

Transportation from the Airport: Upon arrival, travelers can easily find ground transportation options such as taxis, rideshare services like Uber and Lyft, airport shuttles, and car rental services to reach their accommodations or explore the city.

Driving to Austin

For those traveling within Texas or nearby states, driving to Austin can be a convenient option, offering flexibility and the opportunity to explore the scenic routes. Here are some considerations for driving to Austin:

Interstate Highways: Austin is accessible via major highways, including Interstate 35 (I-35) from the north and south, Interstate 10 (I-10) from the west, and Interstate 45 (I-45) from the east. These highways provide easy access to the city from neighboring states like Oklahoma, Louisiana, and New Mexico.

Scenic Routes: Travelers can also opt for scenic routes, such as the Texas Hill Country Drive, which offers picturesque landscapes and charming towns along the way.

Parking: Parking options in Austin include street parking, public parking garages, and designated parking lots. However, downtown Austin can experience high demand for parking during peak times and events, so it's advisable to plan parking arrangements in advance.

Taking the Bus or Train

For those looking for alternative transportation methods or eco-friendly options, there are bus and train services available to reach Austin:

Greyhound and Megabus: Greyhound and Megabus operate intercity bus services with routes connecting major cities to

Austin. These buses offer affordable fares and convenient schedules for travelers.

Amtrak: While Amtrak does not have direct routes to Austin, travelers can take Amtrak trains to nearby cities like San Antonio or Dallas and then use connecting bus services to reach Austin.

Cycling and Walking
Austin is a bike-friendly city with numerous bike lanes and trails, making cycling a popular mode of transportation, especially for short distances within the city center. Additionally, downtown Austin is pedestrian-friendly, allowing visitors to explore attractions on foot easily.

Rideshare Services and Taxis
Rideshare services like Uber and Lyft are widely available in Austin, offering convenient and on-demand transportation options for getting around the city. Traditional taxis are also accessible for those preferring a more traditional mode of transport.

Renting a Car
Renting a car is a popular choice for travelers who prefer the flexibility of exploring Austin and its surrounding areas at their own pace. Multiple car rental companies operate in Austin, providing a range of vehicle options to suit different preferences and budgets.

Where to Stay (Accommodation Guide)

When planning a trip to Austin, Texas, choosing the right accommodation is crucial to ensuring a comfortable and enjoyable stay. Austin is a vibrant city with diverse neighborhoods, each offering unique experiences and accommodations. Whether you prefer luxury hotels, cozy bed and breakfasts, or budget-friendly options, Austin has something for every traveler.

Downtown Austin

Luxury Hotels: Downtown Austin boasts several luxury hotels that cater to discerning travelers. The Fairmont Austin, located near the Convention Center, offers elegant rooms with stunning city views, a rooftop pool, and upscale dining options. The Driskill Hotel, a historic landmark, combines classic charm with modern amenities, making it a favorite among luxury travelers.

Boutique Hotels: For those seeking a unique and stylish experience, boutique hotels in downtown Austin are a great choice. Hotel Ella, a boutique hotel housed in a beautifully restored mansion, offers luxurious rooms, a cozy courtyard, and proximity to downtown attractions. The LINE Austin is another boutique gem known for its artistic flair, waterfront location, and trendy rooftop bar.

Mid-Range Options: Travelers looking for comfortable yet affordable accommodations will find plenty of mid-range hotels in downtown Austin. The Aloft Austin Downtown, with its modern design and lively atmosphere, is a popular choice among young professionals and leisure travelers. The Westin Austin Downtown is another mid-range option offering spacious rooms, a rooftop pool, and easy access to downtown attractions.

Alternative Lodging: In addition to traditional hotels, downtown Austin also offers alternative lodging options such as Airbnb rentals and boutique hostels. These options provide a more local and immersive experience, allowing travelers to stay in trendy neighborhoods like East Austin or South Congress.

South Congress (SoCo)

Eclectic Lodging: South Congress, known for its eclectic shops, vibrant nightlife, and iconic street art, offers a range of unique lodging options. The South Congress Hotel combines modern luxury with Austin's laid-back vibe, featuring stylish rooms, a rooftop pool, and trendy restaurants. The Austin Motel, a retro-chic motel with colorful decor and a lively atmosphere, is perfect for travelers seeking a fun and quirky stay.

Bed and Breakfasts: South Congress is also home to charming bed and breakfasts that provide a cozy and intimate experience. The Kimber Modern, a boutique bed and breakfast with sleek design and personalized service, offers a tranquil retreat in the heart of SoCo. The Brava House Bed and Breakfast is another charming option known for its historic charm, homemade breakfasts, and welcoming hospitality.

East Austin

Hip and Trendy: East Austin has emerged as a hip and trendy neighborhood with a thriving arts and music scene. The LINE Austin, mentioned earlier, is a standout hotel in this area, offering stylish accommodations and waterfront views. The Native Hostel, a boutique hostel and event space, attracts a young and creative crowd with its artistic vibe, live music events, and communal spaces.

Unique Stays: In East Austin, travelers can also find unique stays such as converted lofts, artist studios, and boutique guesthouses. These accommodations reflect the neighborhood's creative spirit and offer a one-of-a-kind experience for adventurous travelers.

North Austin

Family-Friendly Options: North Austin is ideal for families and business travelers looking for a quieter and more suburban setting. Hotels like the Renaissance Austin Hotel offer spacious rooms, family-friendly amenities, and easy access to attractions like the Domain shopping center and the Arboretum.

Extended Stay: Travelers planning a longer stay in Austin will find plenty of extended stay hotels and serviced apartments in North Austin. These accommodations provide the comforts of home, including fully equipped kitchens, laundry facilities, and separate living areas.

Budget-Friendly Choices

Motels and Budget Hotels: For budget-conscious travelers, Austin has a range of motels and budget hotels offering affordable rates without compromising on comfort. Chains like Motel 6, Super 8, and Best Western are scattered throughout the city, providing convenient and wallet-friendly options for accommodation.

Hostels and Shared Accommodations: Hostels and shared accommodations are also great choices for budget travelers, especially those looking to meet fellow travelers and experience Austin's lively atmosphere. HI Austin Hostel, located near Lady Bird Lake, offers dormitory-style rooms, communal spaces, and outdoor activities for guests on a budget.

Budgeting and Cost of Living in Austin

Cost of Accommodation

Austin offers a wide range of accommodation options to suit different budgets. From luxury hotels to budget-friendly hostels and cozy Airbnb rentals, you'll find plenty of choices. The cost of accommodation can vary significantly depending on factors such as location, amenities, and the time of year.

Luxury Hotels: Expect to pay between $200 to $500 or more per night for upscale hotels in downtown Austin or near popular attractions like the University of Texas at Austin.

Mid-Range Hotels: Mid-range hotels and boutique accommodations typically range from $100 to $200 per night, offering comfortable stays with good amenities.

Budget Accommodations: If you're looking for budget options, consider hostels, motels, or Airbnb rentals. Prices can start as low as $50 to $100 per night, especially if you're willing to stay a bit farther from the city center.

Transportation Costs
Getting around Austin is relatively easy, thanks to its well-connected public transportation system, rideshare services, and bike-friendly infrastructure. Here's an overview of transportation costs:

Public Transit: Capital Metro provides bus and commuter rail services in Austin. Fares typically range from $1.25 for a single ride on the bus to $3.50 for a day pass. The MetroRail offers convenient connections between downtown and suburbs.

Rideshare Services: Expect to pay varying rates for rideshare services like Uber and Lyft, depending on the distance and demand. Short trips within the city may cost around $10 to $20.

Biking and Scooter Rentals: Austin has a bike-sharing program and scooter rentals available, with rates starting at around $1 to unlock a bike or scooter, plus additional charges based on usage time.

Dining and Food Costs

One of the highlights of visiting Austin is exploring its diverse culinary scene, from food trucks serving tacos to upscale restaurants offering gourmet cuisine. Here's what you can expect in terms of dining costs:

Casual Dining: Enjoying a meal at a casual restaurant or food truck can cost anywhere from $10 to $20 per person, depending on the menu and location.

Mid-Range Restaurants: For a nicer dining experience at a mid-range restaurant, budget around $20 to $40 per person, excluding drinks.

Fine Dining: Austin boasts several fine dining establishments where a multi-course meal with wine pairings can range from $50 to $150 per person or more.

Entertainment and Activities

Exploring Austin's entertainment options, from live music venues to outdoor adventures, adds to the overall experience. Here are some estimated costs for popular activities:

Live Music Shows: Ticket prices for live music events vary widely. Expect to pay anywhere from $10 for smaller gigs to $50 or more for concerts at major venues.

Outdoor Activities: Enjoying outdoor activities like hiking in nearby parks or visiting natural attractions may have minimal or no costs, depending on the location.

Museums and Attractions: Admission to museums and attractions like the Bullock Texas State History Museum or the Blanton Museum of Art typically ranges from $5 to $15 per person.

Tips for Budget Travelers

Free and Low-Cost Attractions: Take advantage of Austin's many free attractions, such as hiking trails, public parks, and art galleries offering free admission on certain days.

Happy Hours and Specials: Look out for happy hour deals at restaurants and bars, where you can enjoy discounted food and drinks.

Local Markets and Food Trucks: Explore local markets for affordable souvenirs and try delicious eats at food trucks, which often offer tasty meals at reasonable prices.

Chapter 2:

Accommodation Options

Hotels in different price ranges and locations

Downtown Austin

Downtown Austin is the heart of the city, offering convenient access to iconic landmarks, lively nightlife, and cultural attractions. For those seeking upscale accommodation, there are several renowned hotels to consider:

The Driskill - A historic hotel with luxurious rooms and suites, known for its elegant architecture and prime location on 6th Street.

The Fairmont Austin - A modern luxury hotel offering panoramic views of Lady Bird Lake and the city skyline, featuring upscale amenities and world-class dining options.

The JW Marriott Austin - A sophisticated hotel with spacious rooms, rooftop pool, and proximity to the Austin Convention Center and popular entertainment venues.

For travelers on a budget, downtown also offers affordable options such as:

Holiday Inn Express & Suites Austin Downtown - Comfortable rooms with complimentary breakfast, within walking distance to major attractions like the Texas State Capitol.

Hampton Inn & Suites Austin Downtown - Affordable rates with convenient amenities, ideal for budget-conscious travelers wanting a central location.

South Congress (SoCo)
South Congress is a trendy and eclectic neighborhood known for its vibrant arts scene, boutique shops, and eclectic dining options. Accommodation choices here cater to various preferences:

South Congress Hotel - A stylish boutique hotel offering chic rooms, artisanal dining experiences, and a rooftop pool with views of the city skyline.

Hotel San José - A boutique hotel with a laid-back atmosphere, featuring minimalist design, a courtyard garden, and easy access to SoCo's vibrant scene.

Austin Motel - A retro-style motel with colorful rooms, a popular swimming pool, and a prime location near iconic SoCo boutiques and eateries.

East Austin
East Austin is a dynamic neighborhood known for its creative energy, diverse culinary scene, and cultural attractions. Here, you can find unique and immersive accommodation options:

Native Hostel - A hybrid hostel and boutique hotel offering stylish dormitories and private rooms, social events, and a lively bar scene.

East Austin Hotel - A boutique hotel with modern design, rooftop pool, and proximity to East Austin's art galleries, music venues, and food trucks.

The LINE Austin - A chic hotel housed in a historic building overlooking Lady Bird Lake, featuring contemporary design, on-site dining, and easy access to outdoor activities.

North Austin (The Domain)

The Domain is a bustling district in North Austin known for its upscale shopping, dining, and entertainment options. Accommodations in this area cater to both business and leisure travelers:

Archer Hotel Austin - A boutique hotel with sophisticated rooms, a rooftop pool, and close proximity to The Domain's upscale shopping and dining district.

The Westin Austin at The Domain - A contemporary hotel offering spacious rooms, a fitness center, and easy access to The Domain's vibrant nightlife and cultural attractions.

Aloft Austin at The Domain - A trendy hotel with modern amenities, vibrant decor, and a lively atmosphere, ideal for young travelers and social gatherings.

Austin Suburbs

For those preferring a quieter retreat while still being within reach of Austin's attractions, the surrounding suburbs offer a range of accommodation options:

Hyatt Regency Lost Pines Resort & Spa - A luxury resort located in the scenic Hill Country, offering outdoor activities, spa services, and a peaceful setting.

Omni Barton Creek Resort & Spa - A sprawling resort with golf courses, spa facilities, and panoramic views of the Texas Hill Country, perfect for a relaxing getaway.

Lone Star Court - A boutique hotel in the Domain area offering a blend of retro design and modern amenities, with a courtyard pool and proximity to outdoor recreation areas.

Boutique hotels and unique accommodations

Boutique Hotels

The Driskill
A historic landmark in downtown Austin, The Driskill is renowned for its elegant architecture and luxurious accommodations. With a history dating back to 1886, this boutique hotel offers a blend of Old-World charm and modern amenities.
Amenities: Fine dining restaurants, live music in the evenings, spa services, and proximity to iconic Austin attractions like the Texas State Capitol and Sixth Street Entertainment District.

Hotel Ella
Nestled in the heart of the historic district, Hotel Ella is a boutique hotel known for its sophisticated ambiance and Southern hospitality. The property features beautifully appointed rooms, lush gardens, and exquisite dining experiences.
Amenities: Complimentary breakfast, outdoor pool, fitness center, and easy access to cultural landmarks such as the Blanton Museum of Art and the University of Texas at Austin campus.

South Congress Hotel
Located in the vibrant South Congress Avenue district, this boutique hotel offers a trendy yet laid-back atmosphere. The design-forward rooms, rooftop pool, and stylish dining options make it a favorite among visitors seeking a modern Austin experience.

Amenities: On-site boutiques, artisanal coffee shop, rooftop bar with panoramic views, and proximity to eclectic shops, live music venues, and food trucks on South Congress Avenue.

Kimpton Hotel Van Zandt

Embracing Austin's music culture, Hotel Van Zandt captures the essence of the city's creative spirit. The boutique hotel features music-themed décor, live music events, and a vibrant atmosphere that reflects Austin's dynamic music scene.
Amenities: Live music performances, rooftop pool and bar, pet-friendly policies, complimentary wine hours, and easy access to the Rainey Street Historic District's nightlife.

Unique Accommodations

Airbnb Experiences

For travelers seeking a more personalized and immersive stay, Austin's Airbnb scene offers a plethora of unique experiences. From cozy guesthouses in quiet neighborhoods to stylish lofts in the heart of downtown, Airbnb options cater to various preferences and budgets.
Highlights: Authentic local experiences, diverse accommodation styles, opportunities to connect with Austin residents, and flexibility in choosing locations based on desired neighborhoods and attractions.

Glamping Retreats

Experience the best of nature without compromising on comfort with Austin's glamping retreats. These unique accommodations blend the tranquility of outdoor settings with upscale amenities, offering a luxurious camping experience.
Features: Safari tents, yurts, or cabins nestled in scenic locations like the Texas Hill Country, private decks with panoramic views, outdoor activities such as hiking, stargazing, and campfire evenings with s'mores.

Historic Bed and Breakfasts
Discover Austin's rich history and hospitality at charming bed and breakfast establishments scattered throughout the city. These historic properties often feature elegant Victorian or Texan ranch-style architecture, personalized service, and a cozy ambiance.
Attractions: Gourmet breakfasts prepared with local ingredients, themed rooms reflecting Austin's heritage, serene gardens or porches for relaxation, and proximity to cultural attractions and downtown hotspots.

Ranch and Farm Stays
For a unique Texan experience, consider staying at a ranch or farm just outside Austin. These accommodations offer a retreat into nature, allowing guests to participate in ranch activities, farm-to-table dining experiences, and scenic landscapes.
Activities: Horseback riding, cattle herding demonstrations, organic farm tours, fishing in private ponds or rivers, and evenings spent under starlit skies with barbecue dinners.

Airbnb and vacation rentals

Airbnb in Austin

Overview: Airbnb has become a popular choice for travelers seeking a home-away-from-home experience. In Austin, Airbnb options range from cozy apartments in the heart of downtown to spacious family homes in residential neighborhoods.

Benefits: One of the key advantages of Airbnb is the opportunity to stay in unique properties that reflect Austin's eclectic vibe. Whether it's a modern loft with skyline views or a historic bungalow with a backyard oasis, Airbnb allows you to tailor your stay to your preferences.

Neighborhoods: Austin is known for its diverse neighborhoods, each offering its own charm and attractions. Consider staying in South Congress (SoCo) for its trendy shops and eateries, or explore the artsy vibe of East Austin. Downtown and the University of Texas area are ideal for proximity to nightlife and cultural landmarks.

Budget-Friendly Options: Airbnb offers a range of options to suit different budgets. You can find affordable private rooms for solo travelers or budget-conscious groups, as well as luxury properties for those seeking a more lavish experience.

Local Tips: When booking an Airbnb in Austin, consider factors such as proximity to public transportation, parking availability (especially if you're renting a car), and the host's responsiveness to ensure a smooth and enjoyable stay.

Vacation Rentals in Austin

Types of Rentals: In addition to Airbnb, Austin boasts a variety of vacation rental options, including cottages, townhouses, and even ranch-style properties for a taste of Texas living. These rentals often come with amenities such as kitchens, outdoor spaces, and private pools.

Family-Friendly Accommodations: Traveling with family? Vacation rentals provide ample space for everyone to relax and unwind after a day of exploring Austin's attractions. Look for properties with multiple bedrooms, kid-friendly amenities, and proximity to family-friendly activities.

Pet-Friendly Options: Austin is a pet-friendly city, and many vacation rentals welcome furry companions. Check with the host about their pet policy and any additional fees or restrictions before booking.

Extended Stays: Planning an extended stay in Austin? Vacation rentals offer the comforts of home, including laundry facilities and fully equipped kitchens, making them ideal for longer visits.

Booking Considerations: When booking a vacation rental, consider factors such as cancellation policies, security deposits, and any additional fees for cleaning or amenities. Reading reviews from previous guests can also provide valuable insights into the property and host.

Tips for Choosing Accommodation

Location: Consider your itinerary and prioritize accommodation near your planned activities. Whether you're here for live music, outdoor adventures, or cultural exploration, choosing a central location can enhance your Austin experience.

Amenities: Make a list of must-have amenities, such as Wi-Fi, air conditioning (especially during the hot Texas summers), parking, and accessibility features if needed.

Budget Planning: Set a budget for accommodation early in your trip planning process. Keep in mind that rates may vary depending on the season, special events, and the property's location and amenities.

Host Communication: Communication with your Airbnb host or vacation rental manager is key to a smooth stay. Ask questions before booking to clarify any doubts and ensure that the property meets your expectations.

Local Recommendations: Take advantage of your host's local knowledge. They can recommend hidden gems, restaurants, and activities off the beaten path that you won't find in guidebooks.

Chapter 3:

Exploring Austin Neighborhoods

Downtown Austin

Downtown Austin serves as the heart of the city, offering a mix of historic charm and modern amenities. It is characterized by skyscrapers, cultural landmarks, trendy shops, and a lively atmosphere. Whether you're a history buff, a foodie, a music enthusiast, or someone who appreciates urban exploration, Downtown Austin has something to offer.

Attractions in Downtown Austin

Texas State Capitol: A prominent landmark and the seat of Texas government, the Capitol is a must-visit for its stunning architecture, history, and expansive grounds.

The Contemporary Austin - Jones Center: An art lover's paradise, this museum showcases contemporary artworks and hosts exhibitions, events, and educational programs.

6th Street: Known as the "Live Music Capital of the World," 6th Street is famous for its vibrant nightlife, live music venues, bars, and restaurants.

Lady Bird Lake: Offering scenic views and recreational activities, Lady Bird Lake is perfect for hiking, biking, kayaking, and paddleboarding.

The Moody Theater: Home to Austin City Limits Live, this venue hosts concerts, performances, and events featuring local and international artists.

The Paramount Theatre: A historic theater showcasing films, live performances, and cultural events, preserving Austin's entertainment legacy.

Dining and Culinary Experiences
Downtown Austin boasts a diverse culinary scene, with restaurants, food trucks, cafes, and eateries offering a range of cuisines. From Texas barbecue joints to gourmet dining, here are some dining options to explore:

Franklin Barbecue: Renowned for its mouthwatering brisket and classic barbecue fare, Franklin Barbecue is a must-visit for meat lovers.

Uchi: A sushi aficionado's delight, Uchi serves innovative Japanese dishes with fresh ingredients and creative presentations.

Iron Works BBQ: Family-owned since 1978, Iron Works BBQ serves up delicious ribs, brisket, and traditional Texas barbecue in a rustic setting.

La Condesa: Featuring modern Mexican cuisine and craft cocktails, La Condesa offers a sophisticated dining experience with a vibrant atmosphere.

Gourdough's Public House: Indulge in creative and indulgent gourmet doughnuts at Gourdough's, paired with savory dishes and craft beers.

Nightlife and Entertainment

When the sun sets, Downtown Austin comes alive with a thriving nightlife scene. From live music venues to rooftop bars and clubs, here are some places to experience Austin's nightlife:

The Continental Club: A historic music venue showcasing live performances ranging from blues and jazz to rock and country.

The Rooftop at The Contemporary Austin - Jones Center: Enjoy panoramic views of the city skyline while sipping cocktails and socializing at this rooftop bar.

Bar Peached: Known for its innovative cocktails and Asian-inspired small plates, Bar Peached offers a trendy and relaxed setting for nightlife.

Elysium: Dive into Austin's alternative scene at Elysium, a nightclub featuring DJs, themed events, and a diverse crowd.

HandleBar: With its retro decor, rooftop patio, and lively atmosphere, HandleBar is a favorite spot for dancing, drinks, and good times.

Shopping and Souvenirs

Downtown Austin is dotted with boutiques, galleries, and shops offering unique finds and local products. Whether you're looking for clothing, art, gifts, or souvenirs, here are some places to shop:

2nd Street District: Explore this pedestrian-friendly district for fashion boutiques, art galleries, home decor stores, and specialty shops.

The Domain: A shopping and entertainment complex with a mix of high-end retailers, restaurants, cafes, and outdoor spaces.

South Congress Avenue: Known for its eclectic shops, vintage stores, artisanal crafts, and quirky finds, South Congress Avenue offers a bohemian shopping experience.

Austin Farmers' Market: Browse fresh produce, artisanal foods, handmade goods, and local crafts at the farmers' market for authentic Austin souvenirs.

Transportation and Getting Around

Downtown Austin is easily accessible by various transportation options, including public transit, rideshare services, biking, and walking. Visitors can use apps like CapMetro for buses and trains, as well as rideshare apps for convenient travel within the city center. Additionally, bike rentals and scooter services provide alternative ways to explore Downtown's streets and attractions.

South Congress (SoCo)

History and Culture

To truly appreciate South Congress, it's essential to understand its historical roots and cultural significance. Originally a residential area dating back to the late 19th century, SoCo gradually transformed into a thriving commercial and entertainment district in the mid-20th century. Today, it stands as a testament to Austin's artistic heritage and entrepreneurial spirit.

Shopping and Boutiques

One of the highlights of visiting SoCo is the eclectic shopping experience. Wander along South Congress Avenue, lined with an array of boutiques, vintage stores, and unique shops. Discover handmade crafts, retro clothing, quirky souvenirs, and one-of-a-kind treasures that reflect Austin's creative community.

Music and Entertainment

No trip to Austin is complete without immersing yourself in its renowned music scene, and SoCo doesn't disappoint. Catch live performances at legendary venues like the Continental Club, known for its rockabilly and blues acts, or The Saxon Pub, a favorite among local musicians. From intimate acoustic sets to high-energy concerts, SoCo offers a diverse range of musical experiences.

Food and Dining

Prepare your taste buds for a culinary adventure in SoCo. Explore a variety of dining options, from food trucks serving up gourmet tacos and BBQ to upscale restaurants showcasing innovative cuisine. Indulge in Tex-Mex favorites, savor mouthwatering BBQ ribs, or sample creative dishes prepared by talented chefs using locally sourced ingredients.

Art and Culture

Immerse yourself in the artistic ambiance of SoCo, where street art adorns building facades, galleries showcase contemporary works, and cultural events celebrate creativity. Visit art galleries like Yard Dog Gallery or take a stroll down Graffiti Park at Castle Hill to admire colorful murals and graffiti art.

Outdoor Spaces

Escape the hustle and bustle of the city by exploring SoCo's outdoor spaces. Take a leisurely walk along the scenic trails of nearby parks like Auditorium Shores or relax by the banks of Lady Bird Lake. Rent a bike and explore the neighborhood's charming streets and hidden gems at your own pace.

Events and Festivals

SoCo is a hub of activity throughout the year, hosting a variety of events and festivals that showcase Austin's vibrant culture. Attend the First Thursday celebrations, where local artists, musicians, and food vendors gather for a lively street fair. Experience the South Congress Avenue Bridge Bat Colony, a natural spectacle as thousands of bats take flight at dusk.

Accommodations
For those looking to stay in the heart of SoCo, a range of accommodations are available, from boutique hotels to cozy bed and breakfasts. Enjoy convenient access to the neighborhood's attractions, restaurants, and nightlife while experiencing Austin's hospitality and charm.

Getting Around
Navigating SoCo is easy, whether on foot, by bike, or using public transportation. Explore the neighborhood at a relaxed pace, stopping to admire storefront displays, listen to street musicians, and soak in the vibrant atmosphere. Ride-hailing services and bike rentals are also readily available for convenient transportation options.

Safety Tips
While SoCo is generally safe and welcoming, it's always wise to practice common sense and take precautions when exploring any urban area. Stay aware of your surroundings, keep valuables secure, and follow any local guidelines or recommendations for a hassle-free experience.

East Austin

East Austin's history is deeply rooted in African American and Hispanic communities, contributing to its rich cultural heritage. Over time, this neighborhood has experienced waves of gentrification, leading to a blend of old and new influences. Visitors to East Austin can witness this cultural tapestry through its historic buildings, street art, and community events.

Must-Visit Places

Huston-Tillotson University: Founded in 1875, this historically Black university is a significant landmark in East Austin. Visitors can explore its campus and learn about its contributions to education and culture.

Rainey Street: While technically part of Downtown Austin, Rainey Street borders East Austin and is known for its historic bungalow homes turned into bars, food trucks, and live music venues. It offers a unique blend of old and new Austin vibes.

East Sixth Street: This area of East Austin is bustling with energy, featuring an array of bars, restaurants, and live music venues. It's a must-visit for nightlife enthusiasts looking to experience Austin's vibrant music scene.

HOPE Outdoor Gallery: Formerly known as Graffiti Park, this outdoor art gallery showcases vibrant street art and murals. It's a dynamic space that reflects Austin's artistic spirit and is perfect for Instagram-worthy photos.

George Washington Carver Museum: Located in East Austin, this museum celebrates African American culture and history through exhibits, art collections, and educational programs. It's a meaningful stop for those interested in learning about Austin's diverse heritage.

Dining and Culinary Experiences
East Austin is a food lover's paradise, offering a diverse range of culinary experiences. From food trucks to upscale eateries, visitors

can indulge in delicious dishes representing various cuisines. Some notable dining spots in East Austin include:

Franklin Barbecue: Known for its mouthwatering brisket and long lines, Franklin Barbecue is a must-visit for barbecue enthusiasts.

Sour Duck Market: This casual eatery focuses on locally sourced ingredients and offers a menu that changes with the seasons. It's a great spot for brunch or a relaxed dinner.

Hillside Farmacy: Housed in a historic building, Hillside Farmacy combines a pharmacy-inspired decor with a menu featuring fresh seafood, salads, and creative cocktails.

Veracruz All Natural: For authentic Mexican cuisine, Veracruz All Natural serves up delicious tacos, quesadillas, and fresh juices in a laid-back setting.

Blue Dahlia Bistro: This cozy bistro offers French-inspired dishes using locally sourced ingredients. It's perfect for a romantic dinner or brunch with friends.

Outdoor and Recreational Activities
While East Austin is primarily known for its cultural and culinary scene, it also offers opportunities for outdoor exploration and recreational activities. Visitors can enjoy:

Lady Bird Lake: Bordering East Austin, Lady Bird Lake is a popular spot for kayaking, paddleboarding, and scenic walks along the Ann and Roy Butler Hike-and-Bike Trail.

Roy G. Guerrero Colorado River Park: This expansive park offers hiking trails, picnic areas, and beautiful views of the Colorado River. It's a peaceful retreat within the city.

East Side Murals: Wander through East Austin streets to discover vibrant murals and street art that showcase local artists' talent and creativity.

Boggy Creek Greenbelt: Nature enthusiasts can explore Boggy Creek Greenbelt's trails, wildlife, and native plants, providing a serene escape from the urban hustle.

Nightlife and Entertainment
As the sun sets, East Austin comes alive with a lively nightlife scene. From intimate bars to energetic music venues, there's something for everyone to enjoy after dark. Popular nightlife spots include:

The White Horse: Known for its honky-tonk vibes and live music, The White Horse is a favorite among locals and visitors alike for dancing and good times.

Stay Gold: This cozy bar features live music performances ranging from jazz to indie rock, creating a laid-back and welcoming atmosphere.

Whisler's: A cocktail lover's paradise, Whisler's offers a diverse menu of handcrafted cocktails in a stylish setting with indoor and outdoor spaces.

The Sahara Lounge: With its eclectic decor and diverse lineup of live music, The Sahara Lounge offers a unique experience for music enthusiasts looking to discover new sounds.

Shopping and Local Markets
East Austin showcases a blend of independent boutiques, vintage shops, and local markets, making it a great destination for shopping enthusiasts. Some shopping highlights include:

The East Austin Succulents: This charming shop specializes in succulents, cacti, and plant accessories, perfect for plant lovers and unique souvenirs.

Blue Velvet Vintage: For vintage fashion finds, Blue Velvet Vintage offers a curated collection of clothing, accessories, and home decor items from different eras.

Austin Flea Market: Held periodically, the Austin Flea Market features local artisans, craftsmen, and vintage vendors, offering a diverse range of handmade goods and one-of-a-kind treasures.

West Austin

Historically, West Austin has been an enclave for the affluent and influential, drawing residents and visitors with its scenic beauty and peaceful ambiance. The neighborhood is home to iconic landmarks like the historic Clarksville district, which was established by freed slaves after the Civil War, adding a significant historical layer to the area's charm.

Outdoor Adventures
One of the prime attractions of West Austin is its abundance of outdoor activities. Visitors can immerse themselves in nature at the Barton Creek Greenbelt, a vast expanse of greenery offering hiking trails, rock climbing opportunities, and refreshing swimming holes like the famous Barton Springs Pool. The pool, fed by natural springs, provides a rejuvenating escape from the Texas heat and is a favorite spot for locals and tourists alike.
For those seeking a more leisurely outdoor experience, the Lady Bird Johnson Wildflower Center offers a serene setting to appreciate

native Texan flora and fauna. The center's gardens, trails, and educational exhibits provide a deeper understanding of the region's natural heritage.

Cultural Attractions

West Austin is also home to several cultural attractions that showcase the city's artistic and historical richness. The Blanton Museum of Art, located on the University of Texas at Austin campus, boasts an impressive collection of art spanning diverse cultures and periods. Art enthusiasts can explore exhibitions ranging from classical masterpieces to contemporary works, making it a hub for artistic inspiration.

For a taste of Austin's musical legacy, the Zilker Park area hosts the Austin City Limits (ACL) Live at The Moody Theater, where iconic live performances and music festivals celebrate the city's vibrant music scene. Additionally, the nearby Umlauf Sculpture Garden & Museum offers a serene retreat featuring sculptures by renowned artist Charles Umlauf amidst lush greenery.

Dining and Shopping

West Austin's culinary scene is a culinary delight, with a variety of restaurants offering diverse cuisines to satisfy every palate. From upscale dining establishments showcasing local ingredients to charming cafes serving artisanal coffee, West Austin promises a gastronomic journey filled with flavors and creativity.

The neighborhood's shopping options are equally enticing, with boutique shops, art galleries, and upscale boutiques lining the streets of neighborhoods like Tarrytown and West Lake Hills. Visitors can explore unique finds, handmade crafts, and designer goods while soaking in the relaxed yet refined ambiance of West Austin's retail districts.

Residential Enclaves

While exploring West Austin, visitors can also appreciate the architectural charm and residential diversity of the area. From historic homes in Clarksville to modern estates overlooking the Hill Country, West Austin's neighborhoods offer a glimpse into the city's evolving architectural landscape. The tree-lined streets, spacious yards, and scenic views contribute to the neighborhood's appeal, making it a desirable place to live and visit.

Events and Festivals

Throughout the year, West Austin hosts a range of events and festivals that showcase the community's vibrant spirit and cultural heritage. From music festivals in Zilker Park to art walks in Clarksville, there's always something happening in West Austin to engage and entertain visitors.

Transportation and Accessibility

Getting to and around West Austin is convenient, with major highways like MoPac Expressway (Loop 1) providing easy access to the neighborhood. Visitors can also utilize rideshare services, public transportation options, and bike-sharing programs to explore West Austin's attractions and amenities.

North Austin

North Austin is a vibrant and diverse region that offers a blend of modern amenities, cultural attractions, and natural beauty. From bustling entertainment districts to serene parks and recreational areas, this neighborhood has something to offer for every visitor. Let's dive into the key highlights of North Austin that every tourist should know.

Domain Northside

Domain Northside is a premier shopping and dining destination in North Austin. It features upscale boutiques, renowned retailers, and a variety of restaurants offering diverse cuisines. Visitors can explore trendy fashion stores, luxury brands, and unique shops, making it a paradise for shoppers. Additionally, Domain Northside boasts a lively nightlife scene with bars, lounges, and live entertainment venues.

The Arboretum
Nestled amidst lush greenery, The Arboretum is a picturesque outdoor shopping center known for its scenic beauty and relaxed atmosphere. Visitors can stroll through landscaped gardens, enjoy al fresco dining at charming cafes, and shop at specialty stores offering everything from fashion and accessories to home decor and gifts. The Arboretum is also a great place for family outings, with playgrounds and open spaces for picnics.

Walnut Creek Metropolitan Park
Nature enthusiasts will love exploring Walnut Creek Metropolitan Park, a sprawling green space offering hiking trails, picnic areas, and scenic views. The park is perfect for outdoor activities such as hiking, biking, birdwatching, and nature photography. Visitors can unwind amidst nature's beauty, spot local wildlife, and enjoy a tranquil escape from the city hustle.

The Domain
As one of Austin's most dynamic mixed-use developments, The Domain combines residential living, office spaces, shopping, dining, and entertainment options. It features an eclectic mix of stores ranging from high-end retailers to popular brands, along with diverse dining experiences from casual eateries to fine dining restaurants. The Domain also hosts community events, live music performances, and cultural festivals throughout the year.

Great Hills Park

For those seeking outdoor adventures, Great Hills Park offers scenic trails, panoramic views, and recreational facilities. Visitors can hike through wooded areas, discover hidden waterfalls, and enjoy panoramic vistas of the surrounding landscapes. The park is a haven for nature lovers and provides opportunities for picnics, birdwatching, and wildlife spotting.

North Austin Medical Center
North Austin is home to the renowned North Austin Medical Center, a leading healthcare facility offering a wide range of medical services and specialized treatments. Tourists can rest assured knowing that quality healthcare is easily accessible in this neighborhood, ensuring peace of mind during their stay in Austin.

Tech and Business Hub
North Austin serves as a hub for technology companies, startups, and business ventures. It houses major corporate offices, innovation centers, and coworking spaces, making it an ideal destination for business travelers. Visitors interested in the tech industry can explore cutting-edge developments, attend networking events, and engage with the entrepreneurial spirit of Austin.

Cultural Diversity
One of the unique aspects of North Austin is its cultural diversity. The neighborhood celebrates a blend of cultures, traditions, and cuisines from around the world. Tourists can experience authentic international flavors at ethnic restaurants, discover cultural festivals and events, and engage with a vibrant multicultural community.

Educational Institutions
North Austin is home to several educational institutions, including schools, colleges, and universities. Visitors interested in academic pursuits or cultural exchanges can explore campuses, attend public lectures, and engage with students and faculty members. This aspect

adds a dynamic and intellectual dimension to the neighborhood's identity.

Community Parks and Recreation Centers
In addition to larger parks like Walnut Creek Metropolitan Park, North Austin features numerous community parks, sports facilities, and recreation centers. Tourists can participate in outdoor activities, sports leagues, fitness classes, and community events, fostering a sense of camaraderie and well-being.

Austin Neighborhoods: Hyde Park

History and Heritage
Hyde Park dates back to the late 19th century when it was established as one of Austin's first suburb developments. Its history is deeply intertwined with the growth of the city, reflecting a time when grand Victorian homes and bungalows became synonymous with Austin's expanding urban landscape. Today, many of these historic homes have been lovingly preserved, adding to Hyde Park's timeless appeal.

Exploring the Neighborhood

Shops and Boutiques: One of the highlights of Hyde Park is its eclectic mix of shops and boutiques. From vintage clothing stores to unique art galleries and specialty shops, visitors can spend hours exploring the neighborhood's retail offerings. Don't miss out on the local craftsmanship and handmade goods that reflect Austin's artistic flair.

Hyde Park Bar & Grill: A local institution, the Hyde Park Bar & Grill is a must-visit for food enthusiasts. Known for its classic American fare with a Texas twist, this restaurant captures the essence of Austin's culinary scene. Whether you're craving a hearty burger, Tex-Mex specialties, or a refreshing cocktail, Hyde Park Bar & Grill delivers a memorable dining experience.

Quaint Cafés and Coffee Shops: Hyde Park is dotted with charming cafés and coffee shops, perfect for relaxing afternoons or catching up with friends. Indulge in artisanal coffee, freshly baked pastries, and cozy ambiance as you soak in the neighborhood's laid-back atmosphere.

Parks and Green Spaces: Nature lovers will appreciate Hyde Park's green spaces and parks. Take a leisurely stroll through Patterson Park, known for its lush landscapes, walking trails, and picnic areas. It's a serene retreat within the bustling city, ideal for unwinding and enjoying the outdoors.

Cultural Gems: Hyde Park is home to cultural gems such as the Elisabet Ney Museum, dedicated to the renowned sculptor Elisabet Ney. Explore her historic studio, art collection, and exhibitions that celebrate her legacy and contributions to the arts in Texas.

Community Events: Throughout the year, Hyde Park hosts a variety of community events that showcase its vibrant spirit. From neighborhood festivals to art walks and music performances, there's always something happening in Hyde Park that brings residents and visitors together.

Local Tips and Recommendations

Transportation: Getting to Hyde Park is easy, with convenient access to public transportation and bike-friendly streets. Consider renting a bike to explore the neighborhood at your own pace.

Historic Architecture: Take a self-guided walking tour to admire Hyde Park's historic architecture, from Victorian mansions to Craftsman-style homes. Don't forget your camera to capture the neighborhood's picturesque beauty.

Dining Diversity: Hyde Park offers a diverse culinary scene, from casual eateries to fine dining establishments. Be sure to sample local favorites like barbecue, food trucks, and farm-to-table cuisine for an authentic taste of Austin.

Local Art Scene: Support local artists by visiting galleries and studios in Hyde Park. Discover unique artworks, handcrafted goods, and creative expressions that reflect Austin's dynamic art scene.

Barton Hills

Barton Hills is renowned for its picturesque landscapes, with the iconic Barton Creek running through it. The neighborhood is characterized by lush greenery, rolling hills, and a mix of residential homes, apartments, and condominiums. Its proximity to downtown Austin, coupled with its tranquil ambiance, makes it a desirable destination for visitors seeking a peaceful retreat without sacrificing city amenities.

Barton Hills Attractions

Barton Creek Greenbelt: A nature lover's paradise, the Barton Creek Greenbelt spans over 800 acres, offering hiking trails, swimming holes, rock climbing opportunities, and stunning views of the surrounding wilderness. Visitors can explore scenic spots like Twin Falls, Sculpture Falls, and Campbell's Hole for a refreshing outdoor experience.

Zilker Park: Adjacent to Barton Hills, Zilker Park is a sprawling urban park that hosts various events, festivals, and recreational activities throughout the year. Tourists can enjoy picnics, paddle boating on Barton Springs Pool, attending concerts at the Zilker Hillside Theater, or exploring the Zilker Botanical Garden for a tranquil escape.

Barton Springs Pool: Located within Zilker Park, Barton Springs Pool is a natural spring-fed swimming pool that maintains a cool temperature year-round. It's a favorite spot among locals and tourists alike for swimming, sunbathing, and relaxing amidst the beautiful surroundings.

Barton Creek Greenbelt Trail: This trail system offers a scenic route for hiking, biking, and nature walks. Visitors can immerse themselves in the peaceful ambiance of Barton Hills while exploring the diverse flora and fauna along the trail.

Barton Hills Farmers Market: For a taste of local flavors and artisanal products, the Barton Hills Farmers Market is a must-visit. Open on weekends, the market features fresh produce, handmade crafts, gourmet treats, and live music, providing a vibrant shopping experience.

Barton Springs Road: This bustling thoroughfare is lined with eclectic shops, restaurants, cafes, and bars, offering a mix of cuisines, boutique shopping, and nightlife options. Visitors can sample Tex-Mex delicacies, sip on craft cocktails, or browse through unique boutiques for souvenirs.

Community and Lifestyle
Barton Hills embodies a laid-back yet active lifestyle, attracting residents and visitors alike with its sense of community and recreational opportunities. The neighborhood boasts top-rated

schools, parks, and family-friendly amenities, making it ideal for families and young professionals looking for a peaceful yet vibrant place to call home.

Transportation and Accessibility
Traveling to and around Barton Hills is convenient, thanks to its proximity to major highways, public transportation options, and bike-friendly streets. Visitors can easily access the neighborhood from downtown Austin via car, rideshare services, public buses, or by biking along dedicated bike lanes.

Tips for Visitors

Weather: Austin experiences hot summers and mild winters, so it's advisable to pack accordingly with sunscreen, hats, and light clothing during the summer months, and layers for cooler evenings in winter.

Outdoor Activities: Don't forget to bring comfortable shoes, water bottles, and a sense of adventure to fully enjoy hiking, biking, and outdoor activities in Barton Hills and nearby green spaces.

Local Etiquette: Respect local customs and etiquette, such as keeping trails clean, following park rules, and being mindful of wildlife while exploring nature reserves like Barton Creek Greenbelt.

Exploring Nearby: Consider renting a bike or using rideshare services to explore adjacent neighborhoods like South Lamar, South Congress (SoCo), and Downtown Austin for a comprehensive Austin experience.

Chapter 4:

Top Attractions in Austin

State Capitol Building

The Texas State Capitol Building stands as a symbol of Texas history and government. Completed in 1888, this stunning granite structure is an architectural marvel and a must-visit attraction in Austin. Here's what you need to know about visiting the State Capitol:

History and Architecture: The Capitol's design draws inspiration from the Italian Renaissance style, featuring a majestic dome, grand corridors, and intricate details throughout the building. Guided tours are available to delve deeper into its history, including its role in Texas politics and notable events.

Highlights: Visitors can explore the various chambers, including the Senate and House of Representatives, adorned with historical artifacts and portraits of prominent figures in Texas history. The Capitol's grounds also house monuments commemorating veterans, fallen heroes, and significant milestones in Texas history.

Tours: Free guided tours are offered daily, providing insights into the legislative process, architecture, and notable events that shaped Texas. Visitors can also take self-guided tours and admire the building's exterior, especially during events like sunset when the Capitol is beautifully illuminated.

Visitor Information: The Capitol is open to the public, and admission is free. Plan your visit during weekdays for a chance to witness legislative sessions or attend public hearings. Parking is available nearby, or you can opt for public transportation options to reach the Capitol conveniently.

Events and Activities: Throughout the year, the Capitol hosts various events, from cultural celebrations to educational programs. Keep an eye out for special exhibits, concerts on the Capitol grounds, and opportunities to engage with Texas history and government firsthand.

Tips for Visitors: To make the most of your visit to the State Capitol Building, consider the following tips:

Arrive Early: Beat the crowds by visiting early in the morning or on weekdays.

Dress Comfortably: Wear comfortable shoes for exploring the Capitol's expansive interiors and outdoor spaces.

Bring a Camera: Capture the grandeur of the Capitol's architecture and picturesque views from the grounds.

Respectful Conduct: While exploring the Capitol, maintain a respectful demeanor, especially in areas where legislative proceedings may be ongoing.

Plan Nearby Attractions: Since the Capitol is centrally located, plan to visit nearby attractions like the Bullock Texas State History Museum, Blanton Museum of Art, and the vibrant downtown area.

Lady Bird Lake

Overview: Lady Bird Lake, formerly known as Town Lake, is a scenic reservoir located in the heart of Austin. Named after Lady Bird Johnson, the former First Lady of the United States and a champion of environmental conservation, this lake serves as a peaceful oasis amidst the bustling cityscape of Austin.

Activities and Attractions

Hiking and Biking Trails: One of the most popular ways to experience Lady Bird Lake is by exploring its extensive network of hiking and biking trails. The Ann and Roy Butler Hike-and-Bike Trail, commonly referred to as the "Boardwalk," offers picturesque views of the lake and downtown Austin skyline.

Kayaking and Paddleboarding: Visitors can rent kayaks, canoes, or paddleboards to navigate the calm waters of Lady Bird Lake. This activity is perfect for nature enthusiasts and provides a unique perspective of the city from the water.

Bat Watching: One of Austin's most famous natural spectacles occurs at dusk near the Ann W. Richards Congress Avenue Bridge. During the summer months, millions of Mexican free-tailed bats emerge from beneath the bridge, creating a mesmerizing sight for onlookers.

Picnicking and Relaxation: Lady Bird Lake's shores are dotted with scenic picnic spots and green spaces, making it an ideal location for a leisurely day out with family or friends. Visitors can unwind, enjoy a picnic, or simply soak in the tranquil ambiance of the lake.

Fishing: Anglers can try their luck fishing in Lady Bird Lake, which is home to various fish species, including bass, catfish, and sunfish. Fishing permits may be required, so it's advisable to check local regulations before casting a line.

Events and Festivals: Lady Bird Lake serves as a venue for several events and festivals throughout the year, adding to its allure as a cultural and recreational hub in Austin. From dragon boat races to fitness events and music festivals, there's always something happening at this vibrant waterfront destination.

Environmental Conservation: In addition to its recreational value, Lady Bird Lake plays a crucial role in environmental conservation efforts. The lake and its surrounding green spaces are vital habitats for wildlife and contribute to Austin's reputation as an eco-friendly city committed to preserving natural resources.

Accessibility and Amenities: Lady Bird Lake is easily accessible from various points in downtown Austin, with parking facilities available for visitors. The area is well-equipped with amenities such as restrooms, water fountains, and designated picnic areas, ensuring a comfortable experience for tourists.

Tips for Visitors

Timing: The best time to visit Lady Bird Lake is during the early morning or late afternoon to avoid the midday heat and crowds.

Safety: While enjoying water activities, always prioritize safety by wearing life jackets and following water safety guidelines.

Respect Nature: Help maintain the beauty of Lady Bird Lake by disposing of trash responsibly and respecting wildlife and vegetation.

The Domain (Shopping and Dining)

Situated in North Austin, The Domain stands out as a premier destination for shopping, dining, and entertainment. This upscale outdoor mall boasts a unique blend of high-end retailers, trendy boutiques, and popular dining establishments, making it a must-visit for both locals and tourists alike.

Shopping at The Domain

Luxury Retailers: The Domain is home to an impressive lineup of luxury retailers, including Neiman Marcus, Louis Vuitton, Tiffany & Co., and more. Fashion enthusiasts can indulge in designer shopping experiences and explore the latest trends from top brands.

Boutique Shops: In addition to major luxury brands, The Domain features charming boutique shops offering one-of-a-kind clothing, accessories, and gifts. Visitors can discover unique pieces while supporting local designers and artisans.

Tech and Gadgets: Tech enthusiasts will appreciate the variety of stores specializing in electronics, gadgets, and innovative products. From cutting-edge gadgets to smart home devices, The Domain has something for every tech-savvy shopper.

Home Décor and Furnishings: Those looking to spruce up their living spaces can explore a range of home décor stores at The Domain. From modern furniture to stylish accents, shoppers can find inspiration for interior design projects.

Dining Experiences

Culinary Diversity: The Domain boasts an eclectic dining scene with restaurants offering diverse cuisines from around the world. Whether craving sushi, Italian, Tex-Mex, or classic American fare, visitors can satisfy their culinary desires.

Al Fresco Dining: Many eateries at The Domain feature outdoor seating, allowing guests to enjoy their meals in a scenic and vibrant atmosphere. From casual patio dining to upscale al fresco experiences, there's a dining option for every occasion.

Craft Cocktails and Brews: Beer enthusiasts and cocktail aficionados can explore bars and lounges serving craft brews, signature cocktails, and fine wines. The Domain's nightlife scene comes alive with music, drinks, and lively conversations.

Entertainment and Events

Live Music: Austin is renowned for its live music scene, and The Domain contributes to this reputation with live music performances at select venues. Visitors can enjoy local bands, solo artists, and occasional music festivals throughout the year.

Art Installations: The Domain often features art installations and exhibitions, adding a creative touch to the shopping and dining experience. Art enthusiasts can appreciate unique artworks while strolling through the outdoor mall.

Special Events: From seasonal festivals to holiday celebrations, The Domain hosts a variety of special events that attract both locals and tourists. These events showcase the vibrant culture and community spirit of Austin.

Tips for Visiting The Domain

Parking: The Domain offers ample parking options, including valet services and parking garages. Visitors can also utilize ride-sharing services for convenient transportation.

Shopping Hours: Most stores at The Domain operate from morning until late evening, providing ample time for shopping and exploring.

Dining Reservations: For popular restaurants, it's advisable to make reservations in advance, especially during peak hours and weekends.

Outdoor Activities: The Domain features outdoor spaces and walking areas, ideal for leisurely strolls and enjoying the beautiful Texas weather.

Mount Bonnell

Nestled in the western part of Austin, Mount Bonnell stands tall as one of the city's most beloved natural attractions. Known for its panoramic views of the Colorado River and the surrounding Hill Country, Mount Bonnell is a must-visit destination for nature enthusiasts, photographers, and anyone seeking a tranquil retreat amidst stunning landscapes.

History and Significance
Named after George W. Bonnell, who served as Commissioner of Indian Affairs for the Republic of Texas in the 1830s, Mount Bonnell holds historical significance dating back to the early days of Texas settlement. Its elevated vantage point made it a strategic location for scouting and defense during the Texas Revolution.

Over the years, Mount Bonnell has evolved into a recreational hotspot, drawing locals and tourists alike to its summit for leisure activities, picnics, and awe-inspiring sunsets.

Getting There

Located at 3800 Mount Bonnell Road, Austin, TX, Mount Bonnell is easily accessible by car or public transportation. Visitors can park at designated areas near the base of the hill and follow well-marked trails leading to the summit. The ascent is relatively mild, suitable for individuals of all ages and fitness levels.

Attractions and Activities

Upon reaching the top of Mount Bonnell, visitors are greeted with a panoramic vista that captures the essence of Austin's natural beauty. The expansive views of Lake Austin, the Colorado River, and the lush greenery of surrounding parks create a picturesque backdrop for exploration and relaxation.

Some of the key attractions and activities at Mount Bonnell include:

Scenic Overlooks: Multiple vantage points along the summit offer stunning views of the city skyline, waterways, and rolling hills. Be sure to bring a camera to capture memorable moments against the backdrop of nature's splendor.

Hiking and Nature Trails: Mount Bonnell features well-maintained hiking trails that meander through wooded areas and rocky terrain. Nature enthusiasts can spot local flora and fauna while enjoying a peaceful hike amidst natural surroundings.

Picnic Areas: Several designated picnic spots with benches and tables provide ideal settings for al fresco dining. Pack a picnic basket and savor a meal with loved ones while soaking in the panoramic views.

Sunset Spectacle: Sunset at Mount Bonnell is a spectacle not to be missed. As the sun descends beyond the horizon, the sky transforms into a canvas of vibrant hues, casting a warm glow over the landscape. It's a perfect moment for reflection and appreciation of nature's beauty.

Photography Opportunities: Whether you're an amateur photographer or a seasoned pro, Mount Bonnell offers endless opportunities to capture stunning shots. From sunrise to sunset, each moment presents a unique play of light and shadows that inspire creativity.

Tips for Visitors

Timing: Consider visiting Mount Bonnell during weekdays or early mornings on weekends to avoid crowds and fully immerse yourself in the tranquil ambiance.

Weather Awareness: Check weather forecasts before your visit, especially if planning outdoor activities like hiking or picnicking.

Pack Essentials: Carry water, snacks, sunscreen, and comfortable footwear for a pleasant experience.

Respect Nature: Help preserve the beauty of Mount Bonnell by disposing of trash responsibly and respecting wildlife habitats.

Austin's Murals and Street Art

Hope Outdoor Gallery (Castle Hill)
The Hope Outdoor Gallery, also known as Castle Hill, is an iconic landmark in Austin's street art scene. Located at 11th and Baylor

Streets, this outdoor graffiti park offers a dynamic canvas for local and international artists to showcase their talents. Visitors can witness the evolution of murals as artists continuously paint over existing artworks, creating a vibrant and ever-changing display of creativity. The panoramic view of downtown Austin from Castle Hill adds to the allure of this artistic hotspot.

Baylor Street Art Wall
Adjacent to the Hope Outdoor Gallery, the Baylor Street Art Wall is another must-visit destination for street art enthusiasts. This long stretch of retaining wall is adorned with colorful graffiti and murals, providing a fascinating insight into Austin's urban art culture. Artists frequently refresh the wall with new artworks, ensuring that each visit offers a unique experience. Visitors can stroll along the wall, admire the diverse range of styles, and capture Instagram-worthy photos against this captivating backdrop.

Graffiti Park at Carson Creek Ranch
For those looking to explore street art beyond the downtown area, Graffiti Park at Carson Creek Ranch offers a sprawling canvas for artists to express themselves. Situated near the Colorado River, this expansive outdoor space features graffiti-covered structures, including walls, shipping containers, and abandoned buildings. The industrial setting juxtaposed with vibrant street art creates an intriguing atmosphere that attracts photographers, artists, and curious visitors alike.

South Congress Avenue
As you wander down South Congress Avenue, also known as SoCo, you'll encounter a treasure trove of murals and street art adorning storefronts, walls, and alleyways. From whimsical designs to politically charged messages, the artwork along SoCo reflects Austin's diverse creative community. Highlights include the "I Love You So Much" mural outside Jo's Coffee and the colorful murals near

the Continental Club. Exploring SoCo on foot allows visitors to appreciate the artistic details up close while immersing themselves in the vibrant atmosphere of this iconic street.

East Austin

East Austin boasts a thriving art scene with numerous galleries, studios, and outdoor murals waiting to be discovered. The East Side Art Tour offers a curated experience, guiding visitors through the neighborhood's artistic gems, including murals that celebrate Austin's cultural heritage and showcase contemporary themes. From the iconic "Greetings from Austin" mural to hidden gems tucked away in alleyways, East Austin invites exploration and appreciation of its artistic spirit.

Mexic-Arte Museum

While not strictly street art, the Mexic-Arte Museum deserves a mention for its dedication to showcasing Mexican, Latino, and Latin American art forms. Located in downtown Austin, this museum features exhibitions that highlight cultural narratives, social issues, and artistic expressions from diverse communities. Visitors can explore traditional and contemporary artworks, including murals and installations that offer insights into Austin's multicultural identity.

Art in Public Places

Throughout Austin, the Art in Public Places program integrates art into the city's landscape, creating engaging experiences for residents and visitors alike. From sculptures and installations to murals and interactive artworks, these public art pieces contribute to Austin's visual appeal and cultural vibrancy. The program's diverse projects can be found in parks, libraries, civic buildings, and along urban trails, inviting exploration and appreciation of art in unexpected spaces.

Guided Street Art Tours

For a curated experience and in-depth insights into Austin's street art scene, guided tours are available to lead visitors through the city's artistic hotspots. These tours often include visits to mural sites, interactions with local artists, and discussions on the cultural significance of street art in Austin's creative landscape. Whether walking, biking, or riding in a tour van, participants can gain a deeper understanding of the stories and techniques behind the murals they encounter.

Exploring Austin's Murals and Street Art
As you embark on your journey to discover Austin's murals and street art, keep in mind a few tips to enhance your experience:

Respect the Art and Artists: Street art is a form of expression, so please respect the artwork and the artists who created it. Avoid tagging or defacing existing murals.

Capture Memories Responsibly: While photography is encouraged, be mindful of private property and obtain permission when necessary. Respect the space and surroundings while taking photos.

Engage with the Community: Street art often reflects local culture and narratives. Take time to learn about the stories behind the murals and connect with the artistic community to gain deeper insights.

Explore Beyond the Popular Spots: While iconic locations like Castle Hill and South Congress are must-visits, don't hesitate to explore lesser-known areas and discover hidden gems of street art throughout the city.

Sixth Street Entertainment District

History and Overview
The Sixth Street Entertainment District, often simply referred to as Sixth Street, is a historic and bustling area located in downtown Austin. Its origins date back to the late 1800s when it was known as Pecan Street. Over time, it evolved into a hub of entertainment, with bars, clubs, restaurants, and live music venues lining the street.

Live Music Scene
One of the main draws of Sixth Street is its vibrant live music scene. Dubbed the "Live Music Capital of the World," Austin is home to numerous talented musicians and bands, many of whom perform regularly in the venues along Sixth Street. Visitors can enjoy a wide range of music genres, from blues and country to rock and indie.

Bars and Nightlife
Sixth Street is also renowned for its lively nightlife. The area is dotted with an array of bars, pubs, and clubs, each offering its own unique atmosphere and drink selections. Whether you're in the mood for a craft cocktail, a cold beer, or dancing until the early hours of the morning, Sixth Street has something for everyone.

Food and Dining
In addition to its music and nightlife, Sixth Street is a paradise for food enthusiasts. The district is home to a diverse culinary scene, with restaurants serving everything from classic Texas barbecue to international cuisine. Visitors can indulge in delicious meals, sample local delicacies, and experience the fusion of flavors that Austin is famous for.

Art and Culture

Beyond its musical and culinary offerings, Sixth Street is a hub of art and culture. The area is adorned with colorful street art, murals, and sculptures, showcasing Austin's creative spirit. Visitors can explore galleries, attend art events, and immerse themselves in the city's vibrant arts scene.

Events and Festivals

Throughout the year, Sixth Street plays host to a variety of events and festivals that showcase Austin's cultural diversity and creativity. From music festivals and food fairs to art walks and parades, there's always something exciting happening on Sixth Street. Be sure to check local listings and event calendars to make the most of your visit.

Tips for Visitors

Transportation: Sixth Street is easily accessible by car, public transportation, and rideshare services. Parking can be limited, especially on weekends, so consider using alternative transportation options.

Safety: While Sixth Street is generally safe, especially in the main tourist areas, it's always wise to exercise caution and be aware of your surroundings, especially late at night.

Exploring: Don't limit yourself to just one part of Sixth Street. Explore both the historic West Sixth area, known for its upscale bars and restaurants, and the lively East Sixth area, famous for its eclectic mix of venues and food trucks.

Live Music Schedule: Check out the live music schedule in advance to catch performances by your favorite artists or discover new talents. Many venues offer live music throughout the week.

Texas State History Museum

The Texas State History Museum, also known as the Bullock Texas State History Museum, is located in downtown Austin, just a stone's throw away from the Texas Capitol. It stands as a beacon of Texas pride and houses a vast collection of artifacts, exhibits, and interactive displays that bring the state's history to life. The museum's architecture itself is a marvel, designed to reflect the spirit of Texas with its limestone facade and grandeur.

Exhibits and Galleries

Story of Texas: The heart of the museum lies in its "Story of Texas" exhibit, a captivating journey through the state's past. From the days of early Native American civilizations to Spanish colonization, the fight for independence, and the modern era, visitors can immerse themselves in the diverse narratives that have shaped Texas into what it is today.

Becoming Texas: This exhibit delves into the origins of Texas, exploring its transition from a Spanish colony to an independent republic and eventually joining the United States. It highlights key figures such as Stephen F. Austin, Sam Houston, and the struggles and triumphs of early settlers.

Land, Identity, and Culture: Texas's identity is deeply intertwined with its land and culture. This gallery celebrates the state's natural beauty, including its vast landscapes, wildlife, and the contributions of various cultural groups that have enriched Texas's heritage.

Impact of Technology: A fascinating aspect of the museum is its exploration of how technology has influenced Texas's development. From the oil industry to advancements in transportation and communication, this exhibit showcases Texas's journey into the modern age.

Special Exhibitions: The museum regularly hosts special exhibitions that delve into specific aspects of Texas history, offering fresh perspectives and engaging experiences for visitors. These exhibitions may focus on topics such as art, politics, or cultural movements.

Interactive Experiences
What sets the Texas State History Museum apart is its emphasis on interactive learning. Visitors of all ages can participate in hands-on activities, multimedia presentations, and immersive simulations that make history come alive. From virtual reality experiences to interactive games that test your knowledge of Texas trivia, there's something for everyone to enjoy and learn from.

Educational Programs and Events
For those interested in delving deeper into Texas history, the museum offers a range of educational programs and events. These may include guided tours, lectures by historians and experts, workshops on traditional crafts and skills, and family-friendly activities designed to educate and entertain.

Tips for Visitors

Plan Ahead: The museum can be quite extensive, so it's helpful to plan your visit in advance. Check the museum's website for current exhibits, opening hours, and any special events happening during your visit.

Interactive Guides: Consider using the museum's interactive guides or audio tours to enhance your experience. These guides provide additional information, behind-the-scenes insights, and interactive maps to help you navigate the exhibits.

Accessibility: The museum is committed to accessibility, with facilities and resources available for visitors with disabilities. Be sure to inquire about any specific accommodations you may need during your visit.

Souvenir Shop and Cafe: Don't forget to explore the museum's souvenir shop, where you can find unique gifts, books, and memorabilia related to Texas history. After a day of exploration, relax and refuel at the museum's cafe, offering a variety of refreshments and snacks.

Texas Hill Country Day Trips

Texas State Capitol
One of the first places any visitor to Austin should explore is the magnificent Texas State Capitol. Completed in 1888, it stands as a symbol of Texas history and political power. Take a guided tour to learn about the state's legislative process and admire the stunning architecture, including the impressive rotunda and the famous pink granite exterior.

Lady Bird Lake
Formerly known as Town Lake, Lady Bird Lake is a scenic reservoir located in the heart of Austin. It offers a range of recreational activities such as kayaking, paddleboarding, and hiking along the Ann and Roy Butler Hike-and-Bike Trail. Rent a kayak or a stand-up paddleboard to enjoy the serene waters while taking in views of the downtown skyline.

South Congress Avenue (SoCo)
For a taste of Austin's eclectic and trendy side, head to South Congress Avenue, commonly referred to as SoCo. This vibrant street is lined with boutiques, vintage shops, art galleries, and some of the city's best eateries. Don't miss the iconic "I Love You So Much" mural for a quintessential Austin photo opportunity.

Bullock Texas State History Museum
Immerse yourself in Texas history at the Bullock Texas State History Museum. From the early days of Spanish exploration to the present, the museum showcases artifacts, interactive exhibits, and films that highlight the diverse cultural heritage of the Lone Star State. Explore the Story of Texas exhibit for a comprehensive journey through time.

Zilker Park and Barton Springs Pool
Nature enthusiasts will find paradise at Zilker Park, a sprawling green space that hosts various events and festivals throughout the year. Cool off at Barton Springs Pool, a natural spring-fed pool known for its refreshing waters and scenic surroundings. It's a perfect spot for a relaxing day outdoors.

The University of Texas at Austin
Take a stroll through the beautiful campus of The University of Texas at Austin, home to iconic landmarks like the UT Tower and the LBJ Presidential Library. Visit the Blanton Museum of Art to view an impressive collection of artworks spanning centuries and continents.

Austin's Live Music Scene
No visit to Austin is complete without experiencing its legendary live music scene. From blues and country to rock and indie, the city boasts numerous venues where talented musicians perform nightly. Check out famous spots like the Continental Club, Antone's, and the Broken Spoke for unforgettable live performances.

Food and Drink Experiences

Austin is a paradise for foodies, offering a diverse culinary scene that celebrates both traditional Texan cuisine and international flavors. Indulge in mouthwatering barbecue at Franklin Barbecue or try innovative dishes at acclaimed restaurants like Uchi and Franklin Barbecue. Don't forget to sample craft beers at local breweries and sip on creative cocktails at trendy bars.

Outdoor Adventures

Beyond the city limits, Texas Hill Country beckons with its scenic beauty and outdoor adventures. Consider taking day trips to destinations like Hamilton Pool Preserve, where you can swim in a natural limestone pool, or hike along the trails of Pedernales Falls State Park for stunning Hill Country views.

Wine Tasting

Wine enthusiasts can explore the burgeoning wine scene in Texas Hill Country. Embark on a wine tour to visit vineyards and wineries, sample award-winning wines, and learn about the winemaking process. Places like Fredericksburg and Driftwood are known for their vineyards and picturesque settings.

Austin's Live Music Scene

The State Capitol The Texas State Capitol is a must-visit landmark in Austin. Completed in 1888, it stands as a symbol of Texas history and political power. Visitors can take guided tours to learn about the state's legislative process and explore the beautiful architecture of the building, including the impressive dome and historic chambers.

Lady Bird Lake Formerly known as Town Lake, Lady Bird Lake is a scenic reservoir located in the heart of Austin. It offers a variety of recreational activities such as kayaking, paddleboarding, and hiking along the Ann and Roy Butler Hike-and-Bike Trail. The lake also provides stunning views of the city skyline, making it a popular spot for photography enthusiasts.

Zilker Park Zilker Park is a sprawling urban park that hosts numerous events and activities throughout the year. It is home to the popular Barton Springs Pool, a natural spring-fed pool ideal for swimming and picnicking during the hot Texas summers. The park also features botanical gardens, sports fields, and the Zilker Zephyr miniature train, making it a great destination for families and outdoor enthusiasts.

South Congress Avenue South Congress Avenue, often referred to as SoCo, is a vibrant neighborhood known for its eclectic shops, art galleries, and eateries. Visitors can stroll along the avenue and discover unique boutiques, vintage stores, and local food trucks offering a taste of Austin's diverse culinary scene. Don't miss the iconic "I Love You So Much" mural for a perfect Instagram photo!

The University of Texas at Austin For academic and cultural exploration, a visit to the University of Texas at Austin is highly recommended. The campus boasts impressive architecture, including the UT Tower and the LBJ Presidential Library. Visitors can also attend events at the university, such as concerts, exhibitions, and sporting events, to experience the vibrant campus life.

Bullock Texas State History Museum History enthusiasts will appreciate a visit to the Bullock Texas State History Museum. This museum showcases the rich history of Texas through interactive exhibits, artifacts, and multimedia presentations. From the state's early indigenous cultures to its role in the Civil War and beyond, the museum offers a comprehensive look at Texas history.

The Domain For shopping, dining, and entertainment, The Domain is Austin's premier lifestyle center. This upscale outdoor mall features a wide range of stores, from luxury brands to local boutiques, as well as diverse dining options and entertainment venues. It's a great place to spend a day shopping, dining al fresco, or catching a movie at the cinema.

Austin's Live Music Scene One of Austin's most renowned attractions is its vibrant live music scene. Known as the "Live Music Capital of the World," the city boasts a diverse array of venues and genres, catering to music lovers of all tastes. From iconic venues like the Continental Club and Antone's to outdoor spaces like Auditorium Shores and Zilker Park, there are endless opportunities to experience live music in Austin.

Austin's live music scene is not limited to established venues; you can also find talented musicians performing in bars, cafes, and even on street corners throughout the city. Whether you're into blues, rock, country, jazz, or indie music, Austin has something for everyone.
The city comes alive during music festivals such as South by Southwest (SXSW) and Austin City Limits (ACL), attracting musicians and music enthusiasts from around the world. These festivals showcase both emerging artists and established acts, providing an immersive experience in Austin's vibrant music culture.

South Congress Avenue (SoCo)

SoCo Overview
South Congress Avenue stretches from the Colorado River to Oltorf Street, offering a dynamic blend of history, shopping, dining, and entertainment. It's a hub of creativity and local flair, drawing in crowds with its colorful murals, vintage shops, and iconic landmarks.

Shopping Extravaganza

SoCo is a shopper's paradise, featuring an array of boutiques, galleries, and stores showcasing everything from vintage clothing to handmade crafts and local art. Explore iconic spots like:

Allens Boots: A legendary cowboy boot emporium where you can find an extensive collection of Western footwear.

Lucy in Disguise with Diamonds: A quirky costume shop with an eclectic mix of costumes, vintage clothing, and accessories.

ByGeorge: A high-end boutique offering designer fashion, jewelry, and home decor items.

Parts & Labour: Celebrating local artisans, this store offers unique gifts, apparel, and home goods.

Culinary Delights

SoCo is a gastronomic haven, offering diverse dining options ranging from food trucks to fine dining establishments. Indulge in mouthwatering dishes at:

Home Slice Pizza: Famous for its New York-style pizzas, Home Slice is a must-visit for pizza lovers.

Hopdoddy Burger Bar: Savor gourmet burgers crafted with fresh, locally sourced ingredients and paired with handcrafted beers.

Jo's Coffee: Fuel up with artisanal coffee, pastries, and light bites while enjoying the lively SoCo ambiance.

Perla's Seafood and Oyster Bar: Experience coastal cuisine with a Texas twist, featuring fresh seafood and waterfront views.

Live Music and Nightlife

Austin's reputation as the "Live Music Capital of the World" shines bright on South Congress Avenue. Dive into the vibrant nightlife scene with venues like:

Continental Club: A historic landmark hosting live music performances ranging from blues and rock to country and jazz.

C-Boy's Heart & Soul: A soulful venue with live music, dance floors, and a retro ambiance reminiscent of old-school Austin.

Ego's Lounge: Unwind with karaoke nights and live music in a cozy, dive bar setting loved by locals and tourists alike.

Cultural Landmarks

Explore the cultural heritage of Austin through iconic landmarks on SoCo:

Austin Motel: A retro-chic motel adorned with the iconic "SoCo" neon sign, capturing the essence of Austin's vintage charm.

Bouldin Castle: Discover a whimsical architectural marvel, the Bouldin Castle, showcasing unique design elements and artistic flair.

The Continental Gin Building: A historic site turned creative hub, housing art studios, galleries, and artisanal workshops.

Art and Murals

SoCo's streets are adorned with vibrant murals and artistic expressions, making it a paradise for art enthusiasts and Instagrammers. Don't miss:

Greetings from Austin Mural: An iconic postcard-style mural featuring colorful letters and Austin's skyline, perfect for photo ops.

Willie for President Mural: Pay homage to Texas music legend Willie Nelson with this larger-than-life mural celebrating his legacy.

"I Love You So Much" Mural: Spread love at this famous mural located outside Jo's Coffee, a popular spot for selfies and romantic gestures.

Events and Festivals

SoCo comes alive with various events and festivals throughout the year, adding excitement and cultural richness to the area. Experience:

First Thursday: A monthly event where SoCo's shops and galleries stay open late, offering special deals, live music, and art showcases.

South Congress Avenue Merchants Association (SCAMA) Events: Check out SCAMA's calendar for festivals, markets, and community gatherings celebrating local arts and culture.

SXSW (South by Southwest) Festival: Immerse yourself in the world-renowned SXSW festival, featuring music, film, interactive media, and conferences across Austin, including SoCo.

Getting Around SoCo

Navigating SoCo is convenient, whether you choose to stroll along the bustling sidewalks, rent a bike to explore at your own pace, or hop on a local bus for easy access to neighboring areas. Parking is available, but it can get crowded during peak hours and events, so consider alternative transportation options for a hassle-free experience.

Insider Tips

Plan Your Visit: Check out SoCo's event calendar and plan your visit around festivals or special events to enhance your experience.

Local Recommendations: Don't hesitate to ask locals for recommendations on hidden gems, live music hotspots, and must-try dishes.

Safety and Comfort: SoCo is generally safe, but like any urban area, it's advisable to stay aware of your surroundings, especially at night. Wear comfortable shoes for walking and exploring the area.

The University of Texas at Austin

One of the most iconic landmarks in Austin is the University of Texas at Austin, often referred to simply as UT Austin or UT. Founded in 1883, the university is a major public research institution and a hub of academic and cultural activity.

Campus Tours: Visitors can take guided tours of the UT Austin campus to explore its historic buildings, beautiful grounds, and learn about its academic programs and student life. Tours are offered regularly and provide insights into the university's history and achievements.

Texas Memorial Museum: Located on the UT Austin campus, the Texas Memorial Museum is a must-visit for history and nature enthusiasts. The museum features exhibits on Texas wildlife, geology, paleontology, and Native American artifacts. Visitors can see dinosaur fossils, explore interactive displays, and learn about the natural history of the region.

Harry Ransom Center: For art and literature lovers, the Harry Ransom Center at UT Austin is a treasure trove of rare books, manuscripts, photography, and art collections. The center houses works by renowned authors such as James Joyce, Tennessee Williams, and Gabriel García Márquez, making it a mecca for literary enthusiasts.

LBJ Presidential Library: The Lyndon Baines Johnson Presidential Library and Museum, located on the UT Austin campus, offers a fascinating glimpse into the life and presidency of President LBJ. Visitors can explore exhibits on civil rights, the Vietnam War, and the Great Society programs, as well as view presidential artifacts and documents.

Performing Arts: UT Austin is known for its vibrant performing arts scene, with venues like the Bass Concert Hall hosting a variety of performances including concerts, plays, and dance shows. Tourists can check the university's events calendar for upcoming shows and cultural events during their visit.

Texas Longhorns Sports: Sports fans visiting Austin can catch a University of Texas Longhorns game at one of the university's sports facilities. Whether it's football at Darrell K Royal-Texas Memorial Stadium, basketball at the Frank Erwin Center, or baseball at UFCU Disch-Falk Field, experiencing a Longhorns game is a quintessential Austin experience.

Blanton Museum of Art: Adjacent to the UT Austin campus is the Blanton Museum of Art, showcasing a diverse collection of over 18,000 works ranging from Renaissance paintings to modern art installations. The museum's permanent collection includes pieces by artists such as Diego Rivera, Thomas Hart Benton, and Ellsworth Kelly.

Cactus Garden and Sculpture Garden: The UT Austin campus is home to serene outdoor spaces like the Cactus Garden and Sculpture Garden, perfect for a leisurely stroll amidst desert plants and contemporary art installations.

Educational Programs: UT Austin also offers educational programs and workshops for visitors interested in topics such as history, science, and the arts. These programs provide a deeper understanding of the university's academic offerings and research initiatives.

Shop and Dine at the Drag: Adjacent to the university campus is "The Drag," a bustling stretch of Guadalupe Street lined with shops, restaurants, and cafes. Visitors can browse for UT Austin merchandise, grab a bite to eat, or enjoy a cup of coffee while soaking in the lively college atmosphere.

Zilker Park and Barton Springs Pool

Zilker Park
Zilker Park is a sprawling green space located in the heart of Austin. Spanning over 350 acres, this urban oasis offers something for everyone, from outdoor enthusiasts to families looking for a fun day out. Here are some highlights of what Zilker Park has to offer:

Barton Creek Greenbelt: One of Austin's most beloved hiking and biking trails, the Barton Creek Greenbelt, runs through Zilker Park. Visitors can explore miles of scenic trails, lush vegetation, and stunning limestone cliffs. The Greenbelt is also a popular spot for rock climbing and swimming in natural pools.

Zilker Botanical Garden: Nature lovers will delight in the Zilker Botanical Garden, home to a diverse collection of plants and gardens. Highlights include the Japanese Garden with its serene ponds and bridges, the Rose Garden bursting with colorful blooms, and the Prehistoric Garden featuring ancient plant species.

Zilker Hillside Theater: During the summer months, the Zilker Hillside Theater comes alive with free, open-air performances. From Shakespearean plays to musicals and concerts, this outdoor venue offers a unique cultural experience under the stars.

Austin Nature & Science Center: Located within Zilker Park, the Austin Nature & Science Center is a hands-on educational facility for all ages. Visitors can learn about local wildlife, explore interactive exhibits, and participate in nature programs and guided hikes.

Zilker Park Boat Rentals: For a leisurely day on the water, visitors can rent kayaks, canoes, or stand-up paddleboards at Zilker Park Boat Rentals. Paddle along Lady Bird Lake and enjoy stunning views of the Austin skyline and surrounding nature.

Zilker Park Miniature Train: Perfect for families with children, the Zilker Park Miniature Train offers a scenic ride through the park. The train takes passengers on a loop around Zilker Park, passing by iconic landmarks and lush greenery.

Annual Events: Zilker Park hosts several annual events that draw crowds from near and far. These include the Zilker Kite Festival, Austin City Limits Music Festival, and Blues on the Green concert series, showcasing the city's vibrant arts and music scene.

Barton Springs Pool

Adjacent to Zilker Park is Barton Springs Pool, a natural spring-fed pool that remains a refreshing oasis year-round. Here's what makes Barton Springs Pool a must-visit attraction:

Natural Beauty: Surrounded by lush greenery and towering trees, Barton Springs Pool offers a tranquil escape from the city's hustle and bustle. The clear, spring-fed waters maintain a cool temperature, making it an ideal spot for swimming and relaxation.

Swimming and Recreation: Barton Springs Pool is a popular spot for swimmers of all ages. The pool's expansive size accommodates lap swimmers, families, and recreational swimmers alike. Lifeguards are on duty during designated hours for added safety.

Barton Springs Bathhouse: The historic Barton Springs Bathhouse, built in the 1940s, adds to the charm of this natural wonder. Visitors can use the bathhouse facilities, including showers and changing rooms, for convenience.

Sustainable Practices: Barton Springs Pool is dedicated to environmental conservation and sustainability. The pool's water comes from underground springs, and efforts are made to preserve the surrounding habitat and wildlife.

Night Swimming: During the summer months, Barton Springs Pool offers night swimming sessions under the stars. It's a unique way to experience the pool's serene ambiance and cool waters after sunset.

Educational Programs: The Barton Springs Pool area also features educational programs about the pool's history, geology, and environmental significance. Visitors can learn about the importance of preserving natural springs and ecosystems.

Picnic Areas and Trails: Surrounding Barton Springs Pool are picnic areas, shady groves, and hiking trails, making it a perfect spot for a day of outdoor fun. Visitors can enjoy a picnic lunch, go for a nature walk, or simply relax by the water's edge.

Tips for Visiting Zilker Park and Barton Springs Pool

Parking: Zilker Park has ample parking, but it can fill up quickly during peak times. Consider carpooling or using ride-sharing services foHiking enience.

Pack Essentials: Bring sunscreen, hats, water bottles, and comfortable walking shoes for exploring Zilker Park and Barton Springs Pool.

Check Hours: Both Zilker Park and Barton Springs Pool have varying operating hours depending on the season and weather conditions. Check their websites or call ahead for the latest information.

Respect Nature: Help preserve Austin's natural beauty by disposing of trash responsibly and respecting wildlife and vegetation.

Enjoy the Experience: Whether you're lounging by Barton Springs Pool, attending a concert at Zilker Park, or exploring the trails, take time to soak in the beauty and charm of these iconic Austin attractions.

Chapter 5:

Outdoor Activities

Hiking and Nature Trails

Barton Creek Greenbelt
One of Austin's most iconic outdoor destinations, the Barton Creek Greenbelt spans over 12 miles and offers a variety of hiking trails suitable for all skill levels. From easy, family-friendly paths to challenging routes for experienced hikers, the Greenbelt has it all. Highlights include the stunning Barton Creek, limestone cliffs, and lush vegetation, providing a refreshing escape from the city's hustle and bustle.

McKinney Falls State Park
Located just a short drive from downtown Austin, McKinney Falls State Park is a natural gem waiting to be explored. The park boasts several hiking trails that lead to breathtaking waterfalls, historic sites, and diverse ecosystems. Visitors can choose from trails like the Onion Creek Hike, which offers scenic views of waterfalls and limestone formations, or the Rock Shelter Trail, where you can discover ancient rock formations and learn about the area's rich history.

Wild Basin Wilderness Preserve
For a more secluded and tranquil hiking experience, head to the Wild Basin Wilderness Preserve. This hidden gem features over 2.5 miles of trails that wind through dense forests, meadows, and creeks. Hikers can encounter a variety of wildlife, including native birds, deer,

and butterflies, making it a perfect spot for nature enthusiasts and birdwatchers.

Lady Bird Lake Hike-and-Bike Trail

For those looking for a leisurely stroll or a scenic bike ride, the Lady Bird Lake Hike-and-Bike Trail is a must-visit. This 10-mile loop around Lady Bird Lake offers panoramic views of the downtown skyline, lush parks, and opportunities for birdwatching. The trail is also dog-friendly, making it a favorite spot for locals and visitors alike to enjoy outdoor activities with their furry friends.

Enchanted Rock State Natural Area

While not in Austin proper, Enchanted Rock State Natural Area is worth the short drive for its iconic pink granite dome and stunning panoramic views. Hikers can explore various trails, including the Summit Trail, which leads to the top of Enchanted Rock and rewards adventurers with sweeping vistas of the Texas Hill Country. The park also offers camping opportunities, allowing visitors to extend their outdoor adventure overnight.

Tips for Hiking in Austin

Weather: Check the weather forecast before heading out, as Texas weather can be unpredictable. Wear appropriate clothing and carry essentials like water, sunscreen, and insect repellent.

Trail Etiquette: Respect nature and fellow hikers by staying on designated trails, disposing of trash properly, and yielding to wildlife.

Safety: Be aware of your surroundings, especially in remote areas. Let someone know your hiking plans and expected return time.

Guided Tours: Consider joining guided hiking tours or groups to learn more about the area's flora, fauna, and history while exploring safely with experienced guides.

Water sports on Lady Bird Lake

Introduction to Lady Bird Lake

Lady Bird Lake, formerly known as Town Lake, is a picturesque reservoir located in the heart of Austin. Named after former First Lady Lady Bird Johnson, this lake spans approximately 416 acres and is a focal point for outdoor enthusiasts seeking recreational activities.

Water Sports Offered

Kayaking and Canoeing: Lady Bird Lake is a haven for kayakers and canoeists of all skill levels. Whether you're a beginner looking for a leisurely paddle or an experienced enthusiast seeking a challenge, there are rental services available along the lake's shores. Explore the tranquil waters and soak in the stunning views of Austin's skyline as you glide along the lake.

Stand-Up Paddleboarding (SUP): SUP has gained immense popularity in recent years, and Lady Bird Lake provides an ideal setting for this activity. Rent a paddleboard and test your balance while cruising on the lake's smooth waters. It's a fantastic way to get some exercise while enjoying the outdoors.

Rowing: For those interested in rowing, Lady Bird Lake offers opportunities to join rowing clubs or rent rowboats. Experience the thrill of rowing as you navigate the lake, surrounded by the natural beauty of the Austin landscape.

Bat Watching Tours: One unique activity on Lady Bird Lake is bat watching tours. During certain times of the year, the Congress Avenue Bridge becomes a spectacle as millions of Mexican free-tailed bats emerge at dusk. Join a guided bat watching tour by kayak or boat to witness this incredible natural phenomenon up close.

Rental Services and Facilities
To make your water sports experience seamless, Lady Bird Lake provides various rental services and amenities:

Boat and Equipment Rentals: Numerous rental shops along the lake offer kayaks, canoes, paddleboards, rowboats, and other equipment on an hourly or daily basis.

Launch Points: Convenient launch points are available around the lake, allowing easy access for water sports enthusiasts.

Instructional Classes: If you're new to kayaking, canoeing, or paddleboarding, consider taking instructional classes offered by local outfitters. They provide safety tips, techniques, and guidance to ensure a enjoyable and safe experience on the water.

Picnic Areas: After a day of water sports, unwind at one of the picnic areas near the lake. Enjoy a scenic meal while basking in the beauty of Austin's outdoors.

Safety and Regulations
While enjoying water sports on Lady Bird Lake, it's essential to prioritize safety. Here are some key safety tips and regulations to keep in mind:

Wear a Life Jacket: Always wear a properly fitted life jacket when engaging in water activities, especially if you're not a strong swimmer.

Stay Hydrated: Texas summers can be hot, so carry plenty of water to stay hydrated throughout your water sports adventure.

Follow Navigation Rules: Familiarize yourself with navigation rules and etiquette on the lake to ensure a smooth and safe experience for everyone.

Respect Wildlife: Lady Bird Lake is home to diverse wildlife. Respect their habitats and observe them from a safe distance.

Best Times to Visit
The best times to enjoy water sports on Lady Bird Lake are during the spring and fall seasons when the weather is mild, and the lake is less crowded. Early mornings and weekdays also offer quieter and more serene experiences on the water.

Golf courses and parks

Golf Courses in Austin

Barton Creek Resort & Spa: Nestled in the picturesque Texas Hill Country, Barton Creek Resort & Spa boasts four championship golf courses designed by renowned architects. From the challenging layouts of Fazio Foothills and Fazio Canyons to the scenic beauty of Crenshaw Cliffside and Palmer Lakeside, golfers can enjoy a diverse range of experiences amidst stunning natural surroundings.

Omni Barton Creek Golf Courses: The Omni Barton Creek Resort features four distinct golf courses, each offering a unique golfing experience. With courses designed by legends like Ben Crenshaw,

Arnold Palmer, and Tom Fazio, golfers can enjoy a blend of tradition and innovation coupled with breathtaking views of the Hill Country.

Grey Rock Golf Club: Known for its challenging layout and beautiful oak-lined fairways, Grey Rock Golf Club provides an excellent golfing experience for players of all skill levels. The course's strategic bunkering and undulating terrain make it a favorite among both locals and visitors.

Lions Municipal Golf Course: Fondly known as "Muny" by locals, Lions Municipal Golf Course holds a special place in Austin's golfing history. This historic course, dating back to 1924, offers a classic layout amidst mature trees and scenic views, providing golfers with a nostalgic and enjoyable round.

River Place Country Club: Situated along the banks of the Colorado River, River Place Country Club offers a challenging yet picturesque golfing experience. The course features elevation changes, water hazards, and stunning hill country views, making it a must-visit for golf enthusiasts seeking a memorable round.

Parks in Austin

Zilker Park: Known as Austin's most beloved park, Zilker Park offers a plethora of outdoor activities for visitors. From picnics and hiking trails to paddle boating on Barton Springs Pool, Zilker Park is a hub of recreational opportunities amidst lush greenery and scenic beauty.

Lady Bird Lake Hike and Bike Trail: Stretching around the picturesque Lady Bird Lake, this 10-mile trail is perfect for outdoor enthusiasts looking to bike, jog, or simply enjoy a leisurely walk surrounded by nature. The trail offers stunning views of the downtown skyline, botanical gardens, and wildlife along the lake.

Mount Bonnell: For panoramic views of Austin and the Colorado River, a visit to Mount Bonnell is a must. A short hike up the stairs rewards visitors with breathtaking vistas, making it an ideal spot for photography enthusiasts and nature lovers.

Barton Springs Pool: Located within Zilker Park, Barton Springs Pool is a natural spring-fed pool that remains a refreshing 68-70 degrees Fahrenheit year-round. Visitors can swim, sunbathe, or simply relax by the poolside amidst lush surroundings, making it a popular summer destination.

McKinney Falls State Park: Just a short drive from downtown Austin, McKinney Falls State Park offers hiking trails, waterfalls, and opportunities for fishing and picnicking. The park's natural beauty and serene atmosphere provide an escape from the city's hustle and bustle.

Biking and Cycling Routes

Lady Bird Lake Trail: One of the most iconic and popular biking routes in Austin is the Lady Bird Lake Trail. This scenic trail circles the picturesque Lady Bird Lake, offering stunning views of the downtown skyline, lush greenery, and the tranquil waters of the lake. The trail is approximately 10 miles long and is ideal for cyclists of all skill levels. It's a great way to immerse yourself in Austin's natural beauty while enjoying a leisurely bike ride.

Barton Creek Greenbelt: For those looking for a bit more adventure, the Barton Creek Greenbelt is a must-visit biking destination. This expansive trail system spans over 12 miles and features diverse terrain, including rocky paths, creek crossings, and shaded woodlands. The Greenbelt offers both beginner-friendly trails and more challenging routes for experienced riders. It's also a fantastic spot for wildlife spotting and exploring the natural wonders of Austin.

Walnut Creek Trail: Located in North Austin, the Walnut Creek Trail is a hidden gem for cyclists seeking a mix of urban and natural scenery. This trail winds through wooded areas, open meadows, and along the scenic Walnut Creek. With various loops and interconnected trails, cyclists can customize their ride based on their preferences and skill level. The trail is well-maintained and offers a peaceful escape from the city buzz.

Southern Walnut Creek Trail: Another excellent trail for cyclists is the Southern Walnut Creek Trail, known for its smooth asphalt surface and scenic surroundings. This 10-mile trail is perfect for road biking enthusiasts looking for a longer ride. It's relatively flat with gentle slopes, making it accessible to riders of all abilities. The trail also features rest areas, bike repair stations, and stunning views of the Texas landscape.

Texas Hill Country Ride: For cyclists looking to venture outside Austin, the Texas Hill Country offers spectacular riding opportunities. The rolling hills, vineyards, and charming towns make for a memorable cycling experience. Popular routes include rides to Fredericksburg, Wimberley, and the Texas Wine Country. These longer rides require some endurance but reward cyclists with breathtaking vistas and a taste of Texas hospitality.

Pace Bend Park: Mountain biking enthusiasts will find Pace Bend Park a thrilling destination. Located west of Austin, this park boasts rugged terrain, rocky trails, and panoramic views of Lake Travis. The challenging trails cater to experienced riders seeking adrenaline-pumping adventures. Be sure to bring proper gear and be prepared for technical sections along the trails.

Circuit of The Americas (COTA) Bike Nights: For a unique biking experience, consider participating in Bike Nights at Circuit of The Americas. This world-class racetrack opens its gates to cyclists on select evenings, allowing them to ride on the same track used for Formula 1 races. It's a fantastic opportunity to cycle on a professional track and enjoy the exhilaration of high-speed cycling.

Tips for Biking and Cycling in Austin:

Safety First: Always wear a helmet and follow traffic rules while biking in Austin. Be aware of your surroundings and use hand signals to communicate with other cyclists and motorists.

Hydration and Nutrition: Texas weather can be hot, especially during summer months. Stay hydrated and carry snacks or energy bars for longer rides.

Bike Rentals: If you don't have a bike, don't worry! Austin offers numerous bike rental services, including electric bikes, mountain bikes, and road bikes. You can easily rent a bike for a day or longer to explore the city's cycling scene.

Join Group Rides: Austin has a vibrant cycling community with regular group rides and events. Joining a group ride is a great way to meet fellow cyclists, discover new routes, and enjoy a social biking experience.

Picnic and BBQ Spots

Picnic Spots

Zilker Park: This iconic park isn't just famous for its festivals and events; it's also an excellent spot for a picnic. Spread your blanket

94

near Barton Springs or find a shady spot under the trees. With ample green space and beautiful views, Zilker Park is a favorite among locals and tourists alike.

Lady Bird Lake: Take a leisurely stroll along the Ann and Roy Butler Hike-and-Bike Trail and find a cozy spot along the shores of Lady Bird Lake for a picnic. Watch kayakers and paddleboarders glide by as you enjoy your meal with a scenic backdrop of the downtown skyline.

Mount Bonnell: For panoramic views of the city and the Colorado River, head to Mount Bonnell. While it's a popular spot for sunset viewing, it's also a fantastic place for a picnic during the day. Climb the stairs to the top and find a spot on the grassy knolls to soak in the beauty of Austin.

Mayfield Park and Nature Preserve: This hidden gem offers a peaceful escape with its gardens, ponds, and peacocks roaming around. Pack a picnic basket and spend a relaxing afternoon surrounded by nature and tranquility.

Emma Long Metropolitan Park: If you're looking for a more secluded picnic spot with options for hiking and swimming, Emma Long Park is perfect. Located along the shores of Lake Austin, it's a great place to unwind and enjoy a meal with family or friends.

BBQ Joints

Franklin Barbecue: No Austin BBQ guide is complete without mentioning Franklin Barbecue. Known for its mouthwatering brisket and long lines (which are totally worth the wait), this place is a must-visit for BBQ enthusiasts.

La Barbecue: Another top contender in the BBQ scene, La Barbecue serves up tender ribs, juicy sausage, and flavorful pulled pork. Be sure to try their homemade sides for the full experience.

Micklethwait Craft Meats: This food truck turned BBQ hotspot offers a variety of smoked meats, including turkey, pork ribs, and brisket. Their creative menu and friendly atmosphere make it a favorite among locals.

Terry Black's Barbecue: With a family legacy rooted in BBQ, Terry Black's is known for its traditional Texas-style smoked meats. Grab a tray of brisket, ribs, and sausage, and savor the authentic flavors of Texas BBQ.

Stiles Switch BBQ & Brew: If you're looking for a relaxed vibe and a great selection of beers to go with your BBQ feast, Stiles Switch is the place to be. Their meat platters and sandwiches are sure to satisfy your cravings.

Whether you're planning a picnic in a scenic park or craving some mouthwatering BBQ, Austin offers a diverse range of options to suit every taste.

Chapter 6:

Arts and Culture

Museums and Galleries

The Blanton Museum of Art
Located on the University of Texas at Austin campus, The Blanton Museum of Art stands as one of the foremost art institutions in Texas. It houses over 18,000 works spanning various periods, including Renaissance, modern, and contemporary art. Visitors can admire masterpieces by renowned artists like Rubens, Picasso, and Warhol. The museum's collection also highlights American, Latin American, and European art, providing a comprehensive view of artistic evolution.

The Contemporary Austin
For those interested in contemporary art, The Contemporary Austin is a must-visit destination. With two locations - the Jones Center downtown and Laguna Gloria, a lakeside estate - this institution showcases cutting-edge works by local and international artists. The Jones Center features rotating exhibitions, while Laguna Gloria's outdoor sculpture park offers a serene setting to appreciate art amidst nature.

Mexic-Arte Museum
Delve into Austin's rich cultural heritage at the Mexic-Arte Museum, dedicated to Mexican, Latino, and Latin American art and culture. The museum's diverse collections include traditional folk art, modern interpretations, and multimedia installations. Visitors can immerse

themselves in exhibitions that explore themes of identity, history, and social issues, providing insights into the region's cultural tapestry.

Harry Ransom Center
Literary enthusiasts will find delight at the Harry Ransom Center, a renowned research library and museum at the University of Texas at Austin. Home to extensive collections of manuscripts, rare books, photography, and film, this center offers a glimpse into literary history. Highlights include original manuscripts by writers like Shakespeare, Twain, and Joyce, as well as artifacts from film and performing arts icons.

The Contemporary Black Art Gallery
Dedicated to showcasing the works of African American artists, The Contemporary Black Art Gallery is a space for dialogue, expression, and cultural exploration. Through exhibitions, workshops, and community events, the gallery fosters a deeper understanding of Black artistry and its contributions to contemporary art movements. It's a place where diversity, creativity, and social engagement converge.

Umlauf Sculpture Garden and Museum
Nestled in a tranquil garden setting, the Umlauf Sculpture Garden and Museum celebrates the legacy of Charles Umlauf, a prominent sculptor. Visitors can wander among outdoor sculptures that blend seamlessly with nature, creating a harmonious environment for art appreciation. The museum also houses Umlauf's works, providing insights into his artistic vision and mastery of form.

The Contemporary Print Austin
For lovers of printmaking and graphic arts, The Contemporary Print Austin offers a unique perspective on artistic expression. Featuring works by local and international printmakers, this gallery showcases the versatility and creativity of print media. From traditional

techniques to innovative approaches, visitors can explore a diverse range of prints that push the boundaries of visual storytelling.

The Museum of the Weird

Embrace the quirky side of Austin at The Museum of the Weird, a blend of oddities, curiosities, and paranormal artifacts. From shrunken heads to vintage sideshow memorabilia, this museum invites visitors into a world of bizarre wonders. It's a fun and offbeat experience that adds a touch of whimsy to Austin's cultural landscape.

Austin Art Garage

Support local artists and discover unique treasures at the Austin Art Garage, a gallery and shop showcasing contemporary art from emerging talents. From paintings and sculptures to mixed-media works, the space exudes creativity and originality. Visitors can browse and purchase pieces directly from the artists, making each acquisition a personal connection to Austin's thriving art scene.

Elisabet Ney Museum

Step into the historic studio of sculptor Elisabet Ney at the Elisabet Ney Museum, dedicated to preserving her legacy and contributions to art. The museum houses Ney's sculptures, studio artifacts, and archival materials, offering insights into her artistic process and influences. It's a glimpse into the life and work of a pioneering female artist in Texas history.

Performing arts venues

Paramount Theatre

Located in the heart of downtown Austin, the Paramount Theatre stands as a historic landmark and a hub for performing arts enthusiasts. Built in 1915, this iconic venue hosts a variety of events including concerts, film screenings, stand-up comedy, and theatrical performances. Its grand architecture and timeless charm make it a must-visit for those seeking a blend of history and entertainment.

ZACH Theatre
ZACH Theatre, named after longtime Austin actor Zachary Scott, is a prominent institution in the city's performing arts landscape. With multiple stages offering diverse productions ranging from classic plays to contemporary works, ZACH Theatre is known for its high-quality performances and commitment to artistic innovation. Visitors can experience captivating storytelling and exceptional acting in a modern theater setting.

Bass Concert Hall
As part of the University of Texas at Austin's Performing Arts Center, Bass Concert Hall is a premier venue for large-scale productions and world-class performances. From Broadway musicals to symphony concerts, the hall's state-of-the-art acoustics and spacious auditorium create an immersive experience for audiences. It's a cultural gem where top-tier talent graces the stage year-round.

The Long Center for the Performing Arts
Situated along the picturesque shores of Lady Bird Lake, The Long Center offers a spectacular setting for a wide array of performing arts events. From ballet and opera to contemporary dance and orchestral concerts, this modern venue caters to diverse tastes and ages. The Long Center's outdoor spaces also host outdoor concerts and festivals, providing a dynamic cultural experience.

Vortex Repertory Company
For those seeking avant-garde and experimental theater, the Vortex Repertory Company is a standout destination. This alternative performance space showcases innovative works that challenge

conventional norms and provoke thought. With a focus on interdisciplinary art forms, the Vortex offers an immersive and thought-provoking journey into the realm of experimental theater.

The Paramount Theatre for the Performing Arts

The Paramount Theatre for the Performing Arts is another historic venue in Austin, known for its commitment to showcasing a diverse range of performances. From musicals and plays to comedy shows and dance recitals, the Paramount offers a dynamic lineup of events that cater to a broad audience. Its central location and rich heritage make it a cultural cornerstone of Austin's arts scene.

Dougherty Arts Center

More than just a venue, the Dougherty Arts Center serves as a creative hub for local artists and the community at large. Here, visitors can attend art exhibitions, live performances, workshops, and classes across various artistic disciplines. The center's inclusive approach fosters a vibrant arts community and provides opportunities for both emerging and established artists to showcase their talents.

One World Theatre

Nestled in the scenic hills of West Austin, One World Theatre offers an intimate and enchanting setting for live music performances. Known for its exceptional acoustics and picturesque surroundings, this venue hosts a diverse range of musical genres including jazz, blues, folk, and world music. Concert-goers can enjoy a memorable evening of music in a serene and inviting atmosphere.

Stateside at the Paramount

As an extension of the Paramount Theatre, Stateside at the Paramount is a cozy venue that specializes in showcasing independent films, live music, and theatrical productions. Its intimate setting allows for up-close experiences with performers and a unique perspective on Austin's creative talents. The venue's eclectic programming adds a distinctive flair to Austin's cultural offerings.

Austin Playhouse
Dedicated to presenting classic and contemporary theater works, Austin Playhouse is a local treasure for theater enthusiasts. With a focus on intimate productions that engage audiences on a personal level, this theater company brings stories to life with authenticity and passion. From thought-provoking dramas to lighthearted comedies, Austin Playhouse offers a range of theatrical experiences for visitors to enjoy.

Street art and murals

Exploring Austin's Street Art Scene

Graffiti Park at Castle Hill
Formerly known as the Hope Outdoor Gallery, Graffiti Park at Castle Hill is an iconic spot for street art enthusiasts. Located at 11th and Baylor Streets, this outdoor gallery offers a constantly changing landscape of graffiti and murals. Artists from all over come here to leave their mark, making it a dynamic and ever-evolving space. Visitors can witness the creative process in action and admire the diverse range of styles and messages displayed on the walls.

South Congress Avenue
Strolling down South Congress Avenue, you'll encounter an array of captivating murals adorning the sides of buildings and storefronts. These murals capture the essence of Austin's eclectic vibe, featuring everything from whimsical designs to thought-provoking artworks. Keep an eye out for the famous "Greetings from Austin" mural, a

vintage postcard-inspired piece that has become an iconic photo spot for tourists and locals alike.

East Austin

The East Austin neighborhood is a treasure trove of street art, with its walls serving as canvases for artistic expression. Explore the streets around East Cesar Chavez and East 6th Street to discover an eclectic mix of murals showcasing local culture, social commentary, and creative flair. The vibrant colors and intricate details of these artworks add character to the neighborhood's vibrant atmosphere.

Notable Artists and Murals

Shepard Fairey

Renowned street artist Shepard Fairey, known for his iconic "Obey" designs and the Barack Obama "Hope" poster, has left his mark on Austin with several striking murals. Look out for Fairey's distinctive style featuring bold graphics and powerful messages, often addressing social and political themes.

J Muzacz

Local artist J Muzacz is celebrated for his intricate and vibrant murals that blend elements of nature, culture, and spirituality. His works can be found across Austin, adding a touch of whimsy and wonder to the city's streets.

Jason Eatherly

Specializing in large-scale murals, Jason Eatherly's creations often explore themes of nature, wildlife, and the human connection to the environment. His attention to detail and emotive storytelling make his artworks stand out in Austin's street art scene.

Significance of Street Art in Austin

Street art and murals play a significant role in Austin's cultural landscape, serving as a platform for artistic expression, community engagement, and storytelling. These artworks reflect the city's dynamic and diverse identity, showcasing local talent while also inviting dialogue on social issues and cultural heritage. By exploring Austin's street art scene, visitors gain insight into the city's creative pulse and the artists who contribute to its vibrant artistic tapestry.

Tips for Exploring Street Art

Wear comfortable shoes: Exploring Austin's street art often involves walking and navigating through different neighborhoods, so comfortable footwear is essential.

Respect the art and artists: While enjoying the murals, be mindful of the artists' work and avoid damaging or defacing the artworks.

Capture the moment: Don't forget your camera or smartphone to capture your favorite murals and share them with others.

Join a guided tour: Consider joining a guided street art tour to gain deeper insights into the artworks, artists, and the stories behind the murals.

Chapter 7:

Cultural Experiences

Live Music Scene(Music Venues, Festival)

Music Venues

The Continental Club
Located on South Congress Avenue, The Continental Club is a historic venue that has been showcasing live music since 1957. It's renowned for its intimate atmosphere and diverse lineup of blues, rock, country, and jazz performances. The club's retro ambiance and legendary status make it a must-visit for music aficionados.

Antone's Nightclub
Founded by the late Clifford Antone, Antone's Nightclub is a legendary blues venue that has hosted iconic musicians such as Stevie Ray Vaughan and B.B. King. It continues to be a mecca for blues enthusiasts, offering electrifying performances and a rich musical history.

Mohawk Austin
Situated in the Red River Cultural District, Mohawk Austin is a hip venue known for its eclectic programming, featuring indie rock, alternative, and punk bands. Its indoor and outdoor stages provide dynamic settings for live music experiences, accompanied by a vibrant crowd and creative ambiance.

The Elephant Room
For jazz enthusiasts, The Elephant Room is a hidden gem nestled below street level in downtown Austin. This cozy jazz club hosts talented musicians and offers a laid-back atmosphere perfect for enjoying smooth jazz performances and craft cocktails.

Austin City Limits Live at The Moody Theater
Home to the acclaimed Austin City Limits television show, The Moody Theater is a state-of-the-art venue located in the lively 2nd Street District. It hosts a wide range of musical acts, from established artists to emerging talents, providing a world-class concert experience.

Stubb's Bar-B-Q
Not just a barbecue joint, Stubb's Bar-B-Q is also a beloved music venue known for its outdoor concerts and vibrant atmosphere. Visitors can enjoy delicious Texas barbecue while listening to live music under the open sky, creating a quintessential Austin experience.

Festivals

South by Southwest (SXSW)
One of the most iconic festivals in Austin, SXSW is a convergence of music, film, and interactive media. It showcases a diverse lineup of artists from various genres, along with industry conferences, film screenings, and interactive exhibitions, making it a must-attend event for both music enthusiasts and industry professionals.

Austin City Limits Music Festival (ACL Fest)
Held annually in Zilker Park, ACL Fest is a major music festival that features top-tier artists across multiple stages. From rock and pop to hip-hop and electronic music, the festival offers a wide range of

musical experiences in a scenic outdoor setting, drawing music lovers from across the country.

Blues on the Green
A beloved Austin tradition, Blues on the Green is a free summer concert series held at Zilker Park. It showcases local and national blues artists, providing a family-friendly environment where attendees can relax on the grass, enjoy picnics, and immerse themselves in soulful music under the starlit sky.

Austin Reggae Festival
Celebrating the vibrant reggae music scene, the Austin Reggae Festival brings together reggae artists and enthusiasts for a weekend of rhythmic beats and positive vibes. The festival also supports a charitable cause, making it a meaningful and enjoyable experience for attendees.

Old Settler's Music Festival
Located just outside Austin, the Old Settler's Music Festival offers a blend of roots, Americana, and folk music in a scenic outdoor setting. With multiple stages, workshops, and camping options, it provides an immersive music experience for all ages, celebrating the rich heritage of American music.

Diversity of Genres
Austin's live music scene is renowned for its diversity of genres, reflecting the city's eclectic musical heritage and inclusive spirit. From blues, rock, and country to indie, hip-hop, and electronic music, there's something for every musical taste and preference. Visitors can explore a plethora of venues, from intimate clubs to sprawling outdoor stages, ensuring a dynamic and memorable music experience.

Austin's Food Truck Culture

The History and Evolution of Food Trucks in Austin
Food trucks have been an integral part of Austin's culinary landscape for decades, dating back to the 19th century when chuckwagons served meals to cowboys and ranchers. However, it wasn't until the early 2000s that Austin's food truck scene truly exploded, thanks in part to relaxed regulations and a burgeoning foodie culture.
Today, Austin boasts one of the most vibrant and innovative food truck scenes in the country, with hundreds of trucks offering everything from traditional Tex-Mex fare to global cuisine with a local twist. Many of these food trucks have gained national acclaim, earning spots on prestigious food lists and attracting food enthusiasts from around the world.

Where to Find Food Trucks in Austin
One of the joys of exploring Austin's food truck culture is discovering hidden gems tucked away in unexpected locations. While you'll find clusters of food trucks throughout the city, some areas are renowned for their concentration of culinary delights.

South Congress (SoCo): This iconic Austin street is lined with food trucks offering a variety of cuisines, from BBQ to gourmet doughnuts. It's the perfect place to sample different flavors while taking in the eclectic vibe of SoCo.

Rainey Street: Known for its historic bungalows-turned-bars, Rainey Street also boasts an array of food trucks serving up delicious bites to complement your night out.

East Austin: The east side of Austin is a hotspot for food truck enthusiasts, with clusters of trucks serving up innovative dishes in vibrant settings.

Food Truck Parks: Austin is home to several food truck parks where you can find multiple trucks in one location, making it easy to sample a variety of flavors in one visit.

Must-Try Food Truck Delicacies
No visit to Austin's food truck scene is complete without trying some of the city's signature dishes. Here are a few must-try delicacies:

Breakfast Tacos: A Tex-Mex staple, breakfast tacos are the perfect way to start your day in Austin. Fillings can range from classic bacon and eggs to creative combinations like migas or avocado and black bean.

BBQ Brisket: Austin is renowned for its BBQ, and many food trucks serve up mouthwatering brisket smoked to perfection. Pair it with traditional sides like coleslaw and baked beans for the ultimate BBQ experience.

Gourmet Burgers: From juicy beef patties to vegan-friendly options, Austin's food trucks offer a wide range of gourmet burgers topped with creative ingredients like avocado, bacon jam, or fried eggs.

Tacos Al Pastor: Influenced by Austin's vibrant Hispanic culture, tacos al pastor feature marinated pork cooked on a vertical spit and served with fresh cilantro, onions, and pineapple for a burst of flavor.

Artisanal Ice Cream: Cool off on a hot Austin day with a scoop of artisanal ice cream from one of the city's food trucks. With flavors ranging from classic vanilla to unique creations like lavender honey or whiskey pecan, there's something for every sweet tooth.

Food Truck Events and Festivals

Throughout the year, Austin hosts a variety of food truck events and festivals that celebrate the city's culinary creativity. From food truck rallies to themed festivals focusing on specific cuisines, these events are a great way to immerse yourself in Austin's foodie culture and discover new favorite dishes.

Austin Food Truck Festival: This annual festival brings together food trucks from across the city for a weekend of culinary delights, live music, and family-friendly activities.

Trucklandia: A celebration of food trucks and their unique offerings, Trucklandia features a wide range of cuisines, competitions, and entertainment for food enthusiasts of all ages.

SouthBites: Held during Austin's renowned SXSW festival, SouthBites showcases the best of Austin's food truck scene alongside interactive panels and events exploring food and culture.

Insider Tips for Enjoying Austin's Food Trucks

Try Something New: Don't be afraid to step out of your comfort zone and try dishes you've never experienced before. Austin's food trucks are known for their innovative and creative approach to cuisine.

Follow the Lines: A long line at a food truck is often a sign of delicious food worth waiting for. Trust the locals and fellow foodies when choosing where to eat.

Check Operating Hours: While many food trucks operate late into the night, it's always a good idea to check their hours of operation before heading out to ensure they're open when you arrive.

Craft Beer and Brewery Tours

Austin's craft beer scene has flourished over the years, earning a reputation for producing unique and flavorful brews. From small-batch artisanal breweries to larger operations, there's a wide variety of options for beer enthusiasts to explore. Here are some key aspects of Austin's craft beer culture to consider:

Diversity of Breweries
One of the defining features of Austin's beer scene is its diversity of breweries. Visitors can explore a range of styles and flavors, from hoppy IPAs to rich stouts and everything in between. Some notable breweries to visit include:

Austin Beerworks: Known for their innovative approach to brewing, Austin Beerworks offers a rotating selection of seasonal and flagship beers. Visitors can enjoy their spacious taproom and outdoor seating area.

Hops & Grain Brewery: Committed to sustainability, Hops & Grain Brewery produces a variety of award-winning beers using locally sourced ingredients. Their taproom provides an educational experience on the brewing process.

Jester King Brewery: Located just outside Austin, Jester King Brewery is renowned for its farmhouse ales and barrel-aged beers. The scenic brewery setting adds to the overall experience.

Live Oak Brewing Company: Specializing in traditional German-style beers, Live Oak Brewing Company crafts refreshing lagers and ales. Their beer garden is a popular spot for relaxation and socializing.

Brewery Tours and Tastings

For a deeper dive into Austin's craft beer culture, brewery tours and tastings offer an immersive experience. Many breweries in the area provide guided tours where visitors can learn about the brewing process, ingredients, and history of the brewery. Some tours may include tastings of various beer styles, allowing guests to discover new favorites.

Beer Festivals and Events

Austin hosts several beer festivals and events throughout the year, showcasing local breweries alongside national and international selections. Events like the Austin Beer Week and Texas Craft Brewers Festival are great opportunities to sample a wide range of beers, attend educational sessions, and meet fellow beer enthusiasts.

Beer and Food Pairings

Pairing craft beer with food is an art form in itself, and Austin's culinary scene offers numerous opportunities for beer and food enthusiasts to indulge. Many breweries collaborate with local restaurants and food trucks to create unique pairing experiences, highlighting the complementary flavors of beer and cuisine.

Tips for Enjoying Craft Beer in Austin

Plan Your Brewery Visits: Research breweries in advance and plan your visits based on location and beer preferences. Check their websites or social media for tour schedules and special events.

Consider Brewery Tours: If you're interested in learning more about the brewing process and behind-the-scenes operations, consider booking a brewery tour. Some breweries may require advance reservations.

Try Local Specialties: Don't miss the chance to sample beers that are unique to Austin breweries. Ask for recommendations from brewery staff or try flights to taste a variety of styles.

Respect Brewery Etiquette: While visiting breweries, remember to follow their guidelines for behavior, such as not bringing outside alcohol, respecting other guests, and enjoying alcohol responsibly.

Explore Beer-Related Events: Keep an eye out for beer festivals, tastings, and pairing events happening during your visit. These events offer a dynamic and interactive way to experience Austin's craft beer culture.

Art Galleries and Museums

Austin, Texas, is not only famous for its vibrant live music scene and outdoor activities but also for its rich cultural offerings in the form of art galleries and museums. Whether you're an art enthusiast, history buff, or simply looking to explore Austin's creative side, the city has a plethora of galleries and museums that cater to a wide range of interests. From contemporary art to Texas history, here are some must-visit destinations that every tourist should know about:

Blanton Museum of Art
Located on the campus of the University of Texas at Austin, the Blanton Museum of Art is one of the foremost art institutions in the state. It houses an impressive collection of over 18,000 works of art, spanning from ancient to contemporary pieces.
Highlights of the museum include the Ellsworth Kelly's "Austin," a stunning building designed by the renowned artist, and the extensive Latin American art collection, showcasing the diverse artistic heritage of the region.

Visitors can explore galleries dedicated to European paintings, modern and contemporary art, prints and drawings, and more. The museum also hosts temporary exhibitions that showcase emerging artists and thematic collections.

The Contemporary Austin

Comprising two distinct locations, The Contemporary Austin offers a dynamic and engaging experience for art enthusiasts. The Jones Center, located downtown, features contemporary art exhibitions, installations, and multimedia projects by local and international artists.

The Laguna Gloria campus, situated on the shores of Lake Austin, provides a serene setting for outdoor sculptures, gardens, and rotating exhibitions. Visitors can enjoy guided tours, artist talks, and educational programs that delve into the creative process and artistic vision.

Mexic-Arte Museum

Celebrating the richness of Mexican, Latino, and Latin American art and culture, the Mexic-Arte Museum is a cultural hub in downtown Austin. The museum's diverse collection includes traditional folk art, contemporary paintings, sculptures, and multimedia installations. Through exhibitions and programs, the Mexic-Arte Museum explores themes of identity, heritage, and social justice, offering visitors a deeper understanding of the cultural mosaic that defines Texas and beyond.

The Contemporary Austin

Located in the heart of downtown Austin, The Contemporary Austin's Jones Center is a hub for contemporary art exhibitions and programs. The museum showcases a diverse range of works by local, national, and international artists, spanning various mediums and styles. Visitors can immerse themselves in thought-provoking exhibitions, participate in artist talks and workshops, and explore the intersection of art, technology, and social issues. The Jones Center's dynamic programming ensures that each visit offers a fresh and engaging experience for art enthusiasts of all ages.

Bullock Texas State History Museum
For those interested in Texas history and culture, the Bullock Texas State History Museum is a must-visit destination. Located in downtown Austin, the museum offers immersive exhibits, interactive displays, and multimedia experiences that bring the state's rich heritage to life.
From the early days of Native American settlements to the modern era, the museum traces Texas' diverse history through artifacts, documents, and multimedia presentations. Highlights include the iconic Texas Star Theater, the Story of Texas exhibit, and special exhibitions that delve into specific aspects of Texas history and culture.

Umlauf Sculpture Garden and Museum
Nestled in a tranquil garden setting, the Umlauf Sculpture Garden and Museum showcases the works of renowned sculptor Charles Umlauf and other contemporary artists. The museum's outdoor sculpture garden features over 50 sculptures set amidst native Texas plants and trees.

Visitors can stroll through the serene pathways, admire the art installations, and gain insight into the creative process behind each sculpture. The museum also offers guided tours, educational programs, and special events that celebrate the intersection of art, nature, and community.

Harry Ransom Center
As part of the University of Texas at Austin, the Harry Ransom Center is a treasure trove of literary and cultural artifacts. The

center's collections include rare books, manuscripts, photography, film archives, and art objects spanning centuries of human creativity. Visitors can explore exhibitions that highlight iconic works such as the Gutenberg Bible, original manuscripts by famous authors, vintage photographs, and memorabilia from film and theater productions. The Harry Ransom Center offers a glimpse into the creative process and the enduring impact of art and literature on society.

Austin Art Garage

For a more intimate and eclectic art experience, the Austin Art Garage showcases the works of emerging and established local artists. Located in the vibrant South Congress Avenue district, the gallery features paintings, sculptures, mixed-media pieces, and more. Visitors can browse a diverse range of artistic styles and genres, from abstract and contemporary to figurative and pop art. The Austin Art Garage also hosts artist receptions, pop-up exhibitions, and art sales, providing opportunities for art enthusiasts to connect with the local creative community.

Performing Arts (Theaters, Dance, Comedy)

Theater Scene

Austin's theater scene is a blend of traditional and experimental performances, offering a diverse range of shows for every taste. Here are some key theaters and performance venues to explore:

Zach Theatre: Known for its Broadway-quality productions, Zach Theatre is a must-visit for theater enthusiasts. With two locations, Zach Theatre offers a variety of plays, musicals, and special events throughout the year.

Paramount Theatre: A historic landmark in downtown Austin, the Paramount Theatre hosts a mix of live performances, including concerts, comedy shows, film screenings, and theatrical productions. Its classic ambiance adds to the charm of experiencing live entertainment.

Vortex Repertory Company: For those seeking avant-garde and experimental theater, the Vortex Repertory Company is a hidden gem. Known for pushing boundaries and exploring unconventional themes, their performances are thought-provoking and immersive.

The Long Center for the Performing Arts: This modern venue showcases a range of performances, from ballet and opera to symphony concerts and theater productions. The Long Center's state-of-the-art facilities and stunning views of downtown Austin make it a top choice for cultural experiences.

Austin Playhouse: A cozy theater located in north Austin, Austin Playhouse offers intimate productions of classic and contemporary plays. It's a great place to catch emerging talent and enjoy well-crafted performances in a more intimate setting.

Dance Performances
Austin's dance scene is dynamic, with a mix of traditional, contemporary, and multicultural performances. Here are some highlights for dance enthusiasts:

Ballet Austin: As the city's premier ballet company, Ballet Austin showcases classical ballets as well as innovative contemporary works. Their performances feature world-class dancers and choreographers, captivating audiences with their grace and artistry.

Tapestry Dance Company: Specializing in tap and percussive dance forms, Tapestry Dance Company celebrates the rhythm and energy of dance. From tap masterclasses to full-scale productions, they offer a unique blend of tradition and innovation in the dance world.

Forklift Danceworks: This innovative dance company creates site-specific performances that integrate dance with everyday environments. From dance collaborations with city workers to community-inspired projects, Forklift Danceworks brings dance out of traditional venues and into unexpected spaces.

Esquina Tango Cultural Society: Explore Latin dance traditions at Esquina Tango, where you can attend classes, workshops, and live performances featuring salsa, tango, samba, and more. Immerse yourself in the vibrant rhythms and cultural heritage of Latin America through dance.

Comedy Shows: Laughter and Entertainment
Austin's comedy scene is lively, with venues ranging from comedy clubs to improv theaters. Prepare to laugh out loud at these comedy hotspots:

The Velveeta Room: A favorite among local comedians and visiting acts, The Velveeta Room offers stand-up comedy shows in an intimate setting. Enjoy a night of laughter with a lineup of talented comedians showcasing their wit and humor.

Cap City Comedy Club: For a night of professional stand-up comedy, Cap City Comedy Club is the place to be. With a history of hosting renowned comedians and open mic nights for up-and-coming talent, it's a hub for comedy enthusiasts.

ColdTowne Theater: If you're into improv and sketch comedy, ColdTowne Theater delivers hilarious performances that are spontaneous and engaging. Catch themed shows, improv battles, and comedy workshops for a dose of laughter and creativity.

The Hideout Theatre: Known for its interactive improv shows and storytelling performances, The Hideout Theatre offers a unique comedy experience. Get involved in improvised scenes and witness comedic brilliance unfold in real time.

BBQ joints and Tex-Mex restaurants

BBQ Joints in Austin

Franklin Barbecue
No discussion about BBQ in Austin is complete without mentioning Franklin Barbecue. This iconic establishment, located on 900 E 11th St, has gained legendary status for its tender and flavorful brisket, ribs, and sausage. Be prepared for long lines, but rest assured, the wait is well worth it for a taste of true Texas BBQ perfection.

La Barbecue
Another top contender in Austin's BBQ scene is La Barbecue, situated at 2027 E Cesar Chavez St. Known for their succulent brisket, pulled pork, and inventive sides, La Barbecue offers a relaxed outdoor seating area perfect for enjoying your smoky delights under the Texas sun.

Micklethwait Craft Meats
For a more intimate BBQ experience, head to Micklethwait Craft Meats located at 1309 Rosewood Ave. This food truck turned BBQ sensation serves up a mouthwatering array of meats, including brisket, ribs, turkey, and house-made sausages, alongside creative sides and desserts.

Terry Black's Barbecue

Terry Black's Barbecue, found at 1003 Barton Springs Rd, is a family-owned BBQ joint renowned for its pit-smoked meats and classic Texas BBQ flavors. With a spacious indoor dining area and a tempting menu, Terry Black's is a must-visit for BBQ enthusiasts.

Stiles Switch BBQ & Brew

Located at 6610 N Lamar Blvd, Stiles Switch BBQ & Brew combines traditional BBQ techniques with a modern twist. From their signature beef ribs to smoked turkey and flavorful sides, this spot offers a relaxed atmosphere and a diverse menu sure to satisfy your BBQ cravings.

Tex-Mex Restaurants in Austin

Matt's El Rancho

When it comes to Tex-Mex, Matt's El Rancho is an Austin institution. Situated at 2613 S Lamar Blvd, this family-owned restaurant has been serving up mouthwatering Tex-Mex dishes since 1952. From sizzling fajitas to cheesy enchiladas, Matt's El Rancho offers a taste of authentic Texan flavors.

Güero's Taco Bar

For a casual Tex-Mex dining experience, head to Güero's Taco Bar located at 1412 S Congress Ave. With its vibrant outdoor patio and a menu featuring tacos, enchiladas, and refreshing margaritas, Güero's captures the essence of Austin's Tex-Mex culture.

Fonda San Miguel

For a more upscale Tex-Mex experience, Fonda San Miguel at 2330 W North Loop Blvd offers a refined menu showcasing traditional Mexican dishes with a modern flair. From their seafood enchiladas to their signature mole dishes, Fonda San Miguel is a culinary gem in Austin.

El Alma
Situated at 1025 Barton Springs Rd, El Alma combines stunning views of downtown Austin with innovative Tex-Mex cuisine. Their rooftop patio is the perfect setting to enjoy dishes like their carne asada tacos, ceviche, and refreshing cocktails.

Trudy's Tex-Mex
Trudy's Tex-Mex, with multiple locations including 8820 Burnet Rd, is known for its festive atmosphere and delicious Tex-Mex fare. Whether you're craving queso dip, sizzling fajitas, or their famous Mexican martini, Trudy's is a beloved spot among locals and visitors alike.

Chapter 8:

Food and Drinks

Food trucks and trailers

When it comes to experiencing the vibrant culinary culture of Austin, Texas, food trucks and trailers play a pivotal role. These mobile kitchens are scattered throughout the city, offering a diverse range of cuisines that cater to every palate. From traditional Tex-Mex flavors to innovative fusion dishes, Austin's food trucks and trailers promise a delightful gastronomic journey for every tourist visiting the city.

Food Truck Parks
Start your food truck adventure by exploring some of Austin's popular food truck parks. Places like The Picnic, South Congress Avenue Food Truck Park, and Rainey Street Food Truck Park are hotspots where multiple food trucks gather, creating a lively and dynamic food scene. These parks often have seating areas, live music, and a vibrant atmosphere that adds to the overall experience.

Tex-Mex Delights
One cannot talk about Austin's food trucks without mentioning Tex-Mex cuisine. Dive into the world of mouthwatering tacos, quesadillas, and enchiladas served with a side of flavorful salsas and guacamole. Visit trucks like Torchy's Tacos, Veracruz All Natural, and Mellizoz Tacos for authentic Tex-Mex delights that will tantalize your taste buds.

BBQ on Wheels

Austin is renowned for its exceptional barbecue, and you'll find this savory goodness on wheels as well. Food trucks such as Micklethwait Craft Meats, La Barbecue, and Valentina's Tex Mex BBQ serve up tender, smoky brisket, ribs, and pulled pork that are sure to satisfy any barbecue enthusiast.

Global Flavors

Embark on a culinary journey around the world without leaving Austin. Food trucks offer a diverse range of global cuisines, from Thai and Indian to Mediterranean and Korean. Try the flavorful curries at Dee Dee Thai, the savory kebabs at Kebabalicious, or the spicy kimchi dishes at Chi'Lantro for a taste of international fare.

Vegetarian and Vegan Options

Austin's food truck scene caters extensively to vegetarian and vegan diners. Trucks like The Vegan Nom, Conscious Cravings, and Bistro Vonish specialize in plant-based delights that are creative, flavorful, and satisfying, proving that plant-based eating can be deliciously exciting.

Sweet Treats

Indulge your sweet tooth with delectable desserts and treats from Austin's dessert trucks. From gourmet cupcakes at Hey Cupcake! to artisanal ice cream sandwiches at Coolhaus, there's a dessert truck to satisfy every craving. Don't miss out on unique offerings like gourmet doughnuts, shaved ice, and homemade pies.

Craft Beverages

Complement your food truck feast with refreshing craft beverages. Many food truck parks and individual trucks offer a variety of craft beers, local wines, and artisanal cocktails to pair with your meal. Sip on a cold brew or a creative cocktail while enjoying the vibrant atmosphere of Austin's food truck scene.

Food Truck Festivals and Events
Keep an eye out for food truck festivals and events happening in Austin throughout the year. These gatherings showcase a wide array of food trucks, live music, and entertainment, creating a festive atmosphere where you can sample an abundance of culinary delights in one place.

Food Truck Etiquette
When dining at food trucks, it's important to observe proper etiquette. Be patient during busy times, dispose of your trash responsibly, and tip the staff if you receive excellent service. Embrace the laid-back, communal vibe of food truck dining and enjoy the unique experience it offers.

Exploring Beyond the City Center
While downtown Austin has a plethora of food trucks, don't hesitate to venture into the outskirts and surrounding neighborhoods. You'll discover hidden gems and lesser-known food trucks that offer exceptional cuisine away from the bustling city center.

Craft breweries and cocktail bars

Craft Breweries

Austin Beerworks
Location: 3001 Industrial Terrace, Austin, TX 78758
Highlights: Known for their innovative brews and laid-back atmosphere, Austin Beerworks offers a wide range of beers from IPAs to stouts. Don't miss their Fire Eagle IPA and Pearl-Snap Pilsner.

Tour Information: Check their website for brewery tour schedules and tasting events.

Jester King Brewery
Location: 13187 Fitzhugh Rd, Austin, TX 78736
Highlights: Situated in the scenic Texas Hill Country, Jester King Brewery is famous for its farmhouse ales and sour beers. Enjoy their rustic taproom and outdoor seating area.
Events: Keep an eye on their calendar for special beer releases and farm-to-table dining experiences.

Zilker Brewing Company
Location: 1701 E 6th St, Austin, TX 78702
Highlights: Nestled in the heart of East Austin, Zilker Brewing Company offers a cozy atmosphere and a diverse beer selection. Try their Marco IPA or Coffee Milk Stout.
Tours and Tastings: Join their guided tours to learn about the brewing process and sample their latest creations.

Live Oak Brewing Company
Location: 1615 Crozier Ln, Del Valle, TX 78617
Highlights: Known for their traditional German-style beers, Live Oak Brewing Company has a spacious beer garden perfect for relaxing with friends. Don't miss their Hefeweizen and Pilz.
Brewery Events: Check their social media for live music nights and food truck pop-ups.

Hops & Grain Brewery
Location: 507 Calles St #101, Austin, TX 78702
Highlights: Committed to sustainability, Hops & Grain Brewery produces high-quality beers using eco-friendly practices. Try their Pale Mosaic and Porter Culture.
Taproom Experience: Visit their taproom for rotating taps, brewery tours, and educational beer tastings.

Cocktail Bars:

The Roosevelt Room
Location: 307 W 5th St, Austin, TX 78701
Highlights: Known for its extensive cocktail menu and expert mixologists, The Roosevelt Room offers a sophisticated yet welcoming ambiance. Try their signature cocktails like the Old Fashioned or the Roosevelt Mule.
Events: Attend their cocktail workshops to learn the art of mixology from industry professionals.

Midnight Cowboy
Location: 313 E 6th St, Austin, TX 78701
Highlights: Tucked away in a historic building, Midnight Cowboy is a speakeasy-style bar with a focus on craft cocktails and personalized service. Reservations are recommended.
Experience: Enjoy a unique cocktail journey with their omakase-style menu, where the bartender creates customized drinks based on your preferences.

Whisler's
Location: 1816 E 6th St, Austin, TX 78702
Highlights: Whisler's is a hip cocktail bar known for its creative libations and lively rooftop patio. Don't miss their Mezcal Mule or Lavender French 75.
Live Music: Check their schedule for live music performances and DJ nights to complement your cocktail experience.

Garage Cocktail Bar
Location: 503 Colorado St, Austin, TX 78701
Highlights: With a retro garage theme and a menu of classic and inventive cocktails, Garage Cocktail Bar offers a fun and nostalgic atmosphere. Try their Garage Margarita or Espresso Martini.

Happy Hour: Take advantage of their daily happy hour specials on cocktails and small bites.

The Townsend

Location: 718 Congress Ave, Austin, TX 78701

Highlights: The Townsend combines elegant décor with a refined cocktail menu, making it a favorite among cocktail enthusiasts. Indulge in their Barrel-Aged Negroni or Gin Fizz.

Live Entertainment: Enjoy live jazz and blues performances while sipping on expertly crafted cocktails at The Townsend.

Chapter 9:

Shopping In Austin

Unique boutiques and shops

South Congress Avenue (SoCo)
South Congress Avenue, often referred to as SoCo, is a must-visit destination for anyone looking for eclectic shopping in Austin. This iconic street is lined with an array of boutiques, vintage stores, art galleries, and quirky shops. Here are some highlights:

Allen's Boots: A haven for cowboy boot enthusiasts, Allen's Boots offers a vast selection of Western footwear, from traditional styles to fashion-forward designs.

ByGeorge: For fashion-forward clothing, accessories, and home goods, ByGeorge is a curated boutique showcasing both established and emerging designers.

Uncommon Objects: Dive into a treasure trove of vintage finds, oddities, and collectibles at Uncommon Objects, where each item tells a unique story.

Feathers Boutique: Known for its bohemian and retro-inspired fashion, Feathers Boutique offers a curated collection of clothing, jewelry, and accessories.

Lucy in Disguise with Diamonds: Step into this costume and vintage clothing shop for a fun and whimsical shopping experience, perfect for finding unique pieces and accessories.

2nd Street District
The 2nd Street District is a trendy area known for its upscale boutiques, designer stores, and lifestyle shops. Here, visitors can explore a mix of local and international brands in a walkable and vibrant setting. Key shops include:

Byron & Blue: Discover stylish women's clothing, accessories, and home decor at Byron & Blue, known for its chic and contemporary offerings.

TOMS Roasting Co.: Combine shopping with social impact at TOMS Roasting Co., where you can shop for TOMS shoes, apparel, and accessories while enjoying ethically sourced coffee.

Austin Rocks Texas: Embrace the spirit of Texas with a visit to Austin Rocks Texas, offering a range of Texas-themed apparel, gifts, and accessories that celebrate the Lone Star State.

Wild About Music: Music lovers will appreciate Wild About Music, a store dedicated to all things music-related, including apparel, accessories, instruments, and unique gifts.

The Domain
For a luxurious shopping experience, head to The Domain, an upscale outdoor shopping center featuring high-end retailers, dining options, and entertainment venues. Here are some standout stores:

Neiman Marcus: Indulge in luxury fashion, accessories, beauty products, and home goods at Neiman Marcus, a premier destination for upscale shopping.

Apple Store: Explore the latest Apple products, accessories, and services at the Apple Store, known for its innovative technology and sleek designs.

Tiffany & Co.: Discover timeless jewelry, watches, and accessories at Tiffany & Co., renowned for its iconic designs and exceptional craftsmanship.

Warby Parker: Find stylish eyewear and sunglasses at Warby Parker, known for its affordable yet fashionable frames and commitment to social responsibility.

Artisan Markets and Pop-Up Shops
In addition to established boutiques and shopping districts, Austin is home to vibrant artisan markets and pop-up shops that showcase local talent and unique finds. Keep an eye out for:

HOPE Farmers Market: Explore a diverse array of locally made goods, including art, crafts, jewelry, clothing, and artisanal foods, at the HOPE Farmers Market, held on Sundays.

Blue Genie Art Bazaar: During the holiday season, don't miss the Blue Genie Art Bazaar, where you can shop for handmade gifts, art, and crafts created by local artists and artisans.

Pop-Up Austin: Stay updated on the latest pop-up shops and markets in Austin, offering a rotating selection of goods ranging from handmade crafts to vintage treasures.

Vintage and Thrift Stores

Feathered Nest

Located in the heart of South Congress Avenue, Feathered Nest is a charming boutique known for its carefully curated collection of vintage clothing, accessories, and home decor. From retro dresses to quirky accessories, this store is a haven for fashion enthusiasts looking for one-of-a-kind pieces.

Blue Velvet

Tucked away in the vibrant East Austin neighborhood, Blue Velvet is a must-visit destination for vintage aficionados. This cozy store features a wide selection of vintage clothing, including denim, graphic tees, and unique statement pieces. The laid-back atmosphere and friendly staff make it a favorite among locals and tourists alike.

Room Service Vintage

If you're searching for vintage home decor and furniture, look no further than Room Service Vintage. Situated on North Loop Boulevard, this store is a treasure trove of retro furniture, mid-century modern pieces, and funky decor items. Whether you're decorating your home or searching for a unique gift, Room Service Vintage has plenty of options to explore.

Buffalo Exchange

With multiple locations throughout the city, Buffalo Exchange is a popular destination for thrift shopping enthusiasts. This resale store offers a mix of vintage and contemporary clothing, shoes, and accessories. Visitors can browse through racks of unique finds and score stylish pieces at affordable prices.

Prototype Vintage Design

For those with a passion for vintage fashion and designer labels, Prototype Vintage Design is a must-visit boutique. Located in the historic SoCo district, this store specializes in high-end vintage clothing and accessories from renowned designers. From vintage

Chanel bags to retro Gucci dresses, Prototype Vintage Design offers a luxurious shopping experience for vintage connoisseurs.

Uncommon Objects

Step into a world of curiosity and nostalgia at Uncommon Objects, an antique and vintage store located on South Congress Avenue. This quirky shop features an eclectic mix of vintage treasures, ranging from antique furniture to whimsical collectibles. Explore the aisles filled with unique artifacts and discover hidden gems waiting to be uncovered.

Goodwill Vintage

Goodwill Vintage, a branch of the renowned Goodwill thrift store chain, offers a curated selection of vintage clothing and accessories. Located on South Lamar Boulevard, this store is a budget-friendly option for those looking to score vintage finds without breaking the bank. Browse through racks of pre-loved clothing and uncover affordable treasures.

Cavalier

Situated in the trendy East Austin neighborhood, Cavalier is a boutique that blends vintage charm with modern style. This store showcases a curated collection of vintage and contemporary clothing, jewelry, and accessories for men and women. From retro-inspired dresses to unique statement pieces, Cavalier has something for every fashion-forward shopper.

Laced With Romance

If you're a fan of vintage-inspired fashion with a rock 'n' roll edge, Laced With Romance is the perfect destination. Located in the heart of downtown Austin, this boutique offers a mix of vintage clothing, accessories, and handmade jewelry. Explore their collection of band tees, leather jackets, and statement accessories for a dose of vintage glamour.

Le Garage Sale

For a unique shopping experience, don't miss Le Garage Sale, a semi-annual event that brings together local boutiques, designers, and vintage sellers under one roof. Held at the Palmer Events Center, this sale offers a wide range of discounted vintage and designer clothing, accessories, and home goods. It's a treasure hunt where you can snag incredible deals on coveted pieces.

When exploring Austin's vintage and thrift stores, keep in mind a few tips to make the most of your shopping experience:

Arrive Early: Some stores, especially during sales events like Le Garage Sale, can get crowded quickly. Arriving early gives you first dibs on the best finds.

Explore Neighborhoods: Austin's vintage scene is scattered across different neighborhoods. Take the time to explore areas like South Congress, East Austin, and North Loop to discover hidden gems.

Be Open-Minded: Vintage shopping is all about embracing unique styles and unexpected finds. Keep an open mind and don't be afraid to try something new.

Inspect Items Carefully: Since vintage pieces often have a history, it's essential to inspect them for any flaws or damages. Look for quality craftsmanship and unique details.

Ask for Recommendations: Don't hesitate to ask store staff or locals for recommendations on the best vintage stores or upcoming sales. They often have insider tips that can enhance your shopping experience.

Farmers' Markets and Artisanal Shops

Farmers' Markets

Sustainable Food Culture: Austin's farmers' markets are more than just places to buy fresh fruits and vegetables; they embody the city's sustainable food culture. Visitors can explore a variety of seasonal produce, artisanal cheeses, homemade jams, and locally sourced meats.

Support Local Farmers: By shopping at farmers' markets, tourists contribute to the local economy and support small-scale farmers and producers. It's a chance to connect with the community and learn about the origins of the food they consume.

Locations and Timing: Some of the most popular farmers' markets in Austin include the Sustainable Food Center Farmers' Market at Republic Square, Barton Creek Farmers Market, and Texas Farmers' Market at Mueller. These markets operate on specific days, usually on weekends, so it's essential for visitors to check schedules beforehand.

Culinary Delights: Apart from fresh produce, farmers' markets often feature food trucks and vendors offering delicious snacks and meals. Tourists can indulge in farm-to-table treats, from gourmet sandwiches to freshly squeezed juices.

Eco-Friendly Shopping: Farmers' markets promote eco-friendly shopping practices by reducing packaging waste and promoting reusable containers. Visitors are encouraged to bring their bags and containers to carry purchases, contributing to a more sustainable shopping experience.

Artisanal Shops

Handcrafted Treasures: Austin's artisanal shops are a treasure trove of handcrafted goods, from unique jewelry and ceramics to bespoke clothing and home decor items. Tourists can find one-of-a-kind souvenirs that reflect the city's artistic flair.

Local Artisans: These shops showcase the work of local artisans and designers, providing a platform for creative talents to thrive. Visitors can meet the makers behind the products and learn about their craft processes.

South Congress Avenue: One of Austin's iconic shopping destinations is South Congress Avenue, known for its eclectic mix of boutiques, vintage shops, and artisanal galleries. Tourists can stroll along the avenue and discover hidden gems.

East Austin Art Scene: The vibrant art scene in East Austin is home to numerous artisanal shops and studios. Visitors can explore art galleries, craft markets, and pop-up shops featuring emerging artists and designers.

Unique Shopping Experience: Unlike mainstream retail stores, artisanal shops offer a unique shopping experience characterized by personalized service, attention to detail, and a sense of discovery. Tourists can engage with the local arts community and take home meaningful souvenirs.

Tips for Shopping in Austin

Plan Ahead: Research farmers' market schedules and artisanal shop locations before your visit to make the most of your shopping experience.

Bring Reusable Bags: Reduce waste by bringing reusable bags and containers for your purchases.

Engage with Artisans: Take the time to talk to artisans and designers to learn about their craft and the stories behind their products.

Explore Neighborhoods: Venture beyond downtown Austin to discover hidden shopping gems in neighborhoods like East Austin, South Congress, and Mueller.

Support Local: Choose to support local businesses and artisans to contribute to Austin's vibrant creative community.

Shopping Malls and Retail Areas

The Domain
Located in North Austin, The Domain is a premier shopping destination offering a mix of upscale retailers, dining options, and entertainment venues. From high-end fashion brands like Louis Vuitton and Tiffany & Co. to popular stores like Apple and Sephora, The Domain caters to discerning shoppers looking for luxury and style. After a day of shopping, visitors can relax at one of the many restaurants or catch a movie at the iPic Theaters.

Barton Creek Square
Situated in Southwest Austin, Barton Creek Square is one of the largest shopping malls in the area. It features a wide range of stores including department stores like Macy's and Dillard's, as well as popular brands like H&M, Gap, and Victoria's Secret. With a diverse selection of shops and eateries, Barton Creek Square is a convenient stop for all your shopping needs.

South Congress Avenue (SoCo)

For a more eclectic and bohemian shopping experience, head to South Congress Avenue, also known as SoCo. This vibrant street is lined with an array of independent boutiques, vintage shops, art galleries, and quirky stores selling everything from cowboy boots to local artwork. SoCo is also famous for its food trucks, live music venues, and unique cultural vibe, making it a must-visit for tourists seeking Austin's alternative scene.

Second Street District

Nestled in downtown Austin, the Second Street District offers a mix of upscale boutiques, specialty shops, and local artisans. Here, you'll find stylish clothing stores, home decor shops, jewelry boutiques, and more. The district also boasts a variety of cafes, restaurants, and bars, making it a great spot for shopping and dining in the heart of the city.

The Arboretum at Great Hills

Combining shopping with scenic surroundings, The Arboretum at Great Hills is an outdoor retail center with a relaxed atmosphere. Visitors can explore a range of stores offering fashion, accessories, home goods, and outdoor gear. The Arboretum's beautiful landscaping, fountains, and walking paths create a pleasant shopping environment where shoppers can enjoy the outdoors while browsing their favorite stores.

Vintage and Thrift Stores

Austin is home to a thriving vintage and thrift store scene, perfect for those seeking one-of-a-kind treasures and sustainable fashion. Places like Room Service Vintage, Buffalo Exchange, and Goodwill Boutique offer a curated selection of vintage clothing, accessories, and home decor items. Exploring these stores not only allows you to find unique pieces but also supports sustainable shopping practices.

Farmers' Markets and Artisanal Shops
Embrace Austin's local flavor by visiting farmers' markets and artisanal shops scattered throughout the city. The Austin Farmers' Market at Mueller and the Texas Farmers' Market at Lakeline are popular destinations for fresh produce, handmade goods, and artisanal food products. Additionally, shops like Blue Genie Art Bazaar and Austin Art Garage showcase the work of local artists, providing a chance to take home authentic Austin creations.

Domain Northside
Complementing The Domain's upscale offerings, Domain Northside features a mix of luxury boutiques, specialty shops, and trendy eateries. Visitors can shop for designer clothing, accessories, beauty products, and home decor items at stores like Kendra Scott, Nordstrom Rack, and Anthropologie. The dining options range from gourmet restaurants to casual cafes, ensuring a well-rounded shopping experience.

Hill Country Galleria
Located in the scenic Hill Country area, the Hill Country Galleria combines shopping with outdoor beauty. This open-air lifestyle center features a diverse range of shops, from national retailers to local boutiques. Visitors can explore clothing stores, gift shops, art galleries, and more while enjoying views of the surrounding hills and green spaces. The Galleria also hosts events, concerts, and farmers' markets, adding to its appeal as a shopping and entertainment destination.

Unique Boutiques and Local Designers
Austin is known for its creativity and independent spirit, reflected in its array of unique boutiques and local designers. Explore areas like East Austin and North Loop for a mix of vintage shops, artisan studios, and fashion boutiques showcasing Austin's homegrown

talent. From handmade jewelry to custom clothing, these shops offer a glimpse into Austin's creative community and provide opportunities to discover distinctive items.

Chapter 10:

Events and Festivals

SXSW(South by Southwest

Overview: SXSW is an annual conglomerate of film, interactive media, and music festivals and conferences that take place in mid-March in Austin. It is one of the largest and most influential events of its kind globally, attracting a diverse range of participants from artists and musicians to tech enthusiasts and industry leaders.

History: The roots of SXSW trace back to 1987 when it began as a music festival. Over the years, it has evolved into a multidisciplinary event encompassing music, film, and technology, making it a mecca for creative minds and innovators.

Segments

SXSW Music: This segment features a vast array of musical performances across various genres, showcasing both emerging artists and established acts. Venues throughout downtown Austin come alive with electrifying concerts, providing an unparalleled music experience.

SXSW Film: A celebration of cinematic creativity, the film segment of SXSW includes screenings of independent films, documentaries, and shorts. It serves as a platform for filmmakers to showcase their work and engage with audiences and industry professionals.

SXSW Interactive: Focused on technology and innovation, this segment attracts entrepreneurs, tech visionaries, and startups from around the world. It features keynote speakers, panel discussions, workshops, and networking opportunities, fostering collaboration and ideation.

Key Highlights

Music Discovery: SXSW is renowned for discovering new music talent. Attendees can explore a diverse range of musical styles and discover their new favorite artists before they hit the mainstream.

Film Premieres: The film segment premieres highly anticipated movies, documentaries, and series, providing a platform for filmmakers to gain exposure and recognition.

Interactive Insights: From cutting-edge technologies to discussions on digital trends, SXSW Interactive offers valuable insights into the future of tech and its impact on various industries.

Tips for Attendees

Plan Ahead: With a multitude of events happening simultaneously, planning your schedule in advance is crucial to make the most out of SXSW. Utilize the official SXSW app for schedules, maps, and updates.

Explore Beyond the Main Venues: While the main venues like Austin Convention Center and Auditorium Shores host major events, don't forget to explore smaller venues and offbeat locations for hidden gems and unique experiences.

Engage and Network: SXSW is not just about attending events; it's also about networking and connecting with like-minded individuals. Attend panels, join discussions, and engage in conversations to expand your professional and social circles.

Survival Tips

Comfortable Attire: Austin's weather in March can vary, so dress in layers and wear comfortable shoes as you'll be walking between venues.

Hydration and Snacks: Stay hydrated, especially if you're outdoors for extended periods. Carry water bottles and snacks to keep your energy levels up.

Transportation: Consider utilizing public transportation, rideshares, or biking to navigate Austin during SXSW, as parking can be challenging.

Notable Past Performances and Events
Iconic musical performances by artists like Prince, Kanye West, Lady Gaga, and The Strokes have graced SXSW stages, creating unforgettable moments.
Film premieres such as "The Hurt Locker," "Bridesmaids," and "Get Out" gained acclaim and buzz at SXSW before achieving widespread success.

Impact on Austin: SXSW has a significant economic and cultural impact on Austin, attracting thousands of visitors and generating revenue for local businesses. It also contributes to Austin's reputation as a hub for creativity, innovation, and artistic expression.

Austin City Limits Music Festival

History and Background
ACL Fest has a rich history, starting in 2002 as an extension of the popular Austin City Limits television show. Over the years, it has grown into a massive event, drawing top-tier artists and creating an immersive experience for attendees.

Dates and Venue
The festival typically takes place over two consecutive weekends in October, offering ample opportunities for visitors to catch their favorite acts. Zilker Park, with its sprawling green spaces and iconic skyline backdrop, provides an idyllic setting for the festival's diverse performances.

Lineup and Performances

ACL Fest boasts an eclectic lineup featuring renowned headliners, emerging artists, and local talent. From rock and pop to hip-hop and electronic music, the festival caters to a broad audience. Past headliners have included iconic acts such as Foo Fighters, Billie Eilish, and Kendrick Lamar, ensuring an unforgettable experience for attendees.

Stages and Atmosphere

The festival grounds are divided into multiple stages, each hosting simultaneous performances throughout the day. From the energetic vibes of the Honda Stage to the intimate settings of the Tito's Handmade Vodka Stage, attendees can explore diverse musical experiences. The festive atmosphere, marked by vibrant art installations, food vendors, and interactive activities, adds to the overall allure of ACL Fest.

Tickets and Passes

To attend ACL Fest, visitors can purchase single-day or weekend passes, with options for general admission and VIP access. Early ticket purchases are recommended, as the festival often sells out due to its popularity. Additionally, ACL Fest offers accommodation packages and shuttle services for convenient access to the venue.

Tips for Enjoying ACL Fest

Plan Ahead: Review the lineup and schedule to prioritize performances you don't want to miss. Consider creating a personalized itinerary to maximize your festival experience.

Stay Hydrated and Sun-Protected: Texas weather can be unpredictable, so dress comfortably and carry essentials like sunscreen and a refillable water bottle.

Explore Beyond Music: In addition to the musical performances, ACL Fest features art installations, local vendors, and interactive experiences. Take time to explore everything the festival has to offer.

Utilize Transportation Options: Consider using public transportation, rideshare services, or shuttle buses to and from the festival to avoid parking hassles.

Respect the Environment: Zilker Park is a cherished green space in Austin, so help keep it clean by disposing of trash responsibly and respecting the natural surroundings.

Beyond ACL Fest
While ACL Fest is a highlight of Austin's festival calendar, the city offers a year-round lineup of events and cultural celebrations. From SXSW (South by Southwest) showcasing film, music, and interactive media to the Austin Film Festival highlighting cinematic talent, visitors can immerse themselves in Austin's vibrant arts scene.

Other annual events and festivals

Austin City Limits Music Festival (ACL): While ACL deserves a mention as one of the biggest music festivals in Austin, it's covered in detail in another chapter. Apart from ACL,

Austin hosts numerous other music festivals that cater to various genres and tastes.

South by Southwest (SXSW): SXSW is an internationally renowned festival that celebrates the convergence of film, music, and interactive media. It's a massive event that takes over the city, featuring film screenings, music showcases, panel discussions, and interactive exhibitions. Attendees get a glimpse of cutting-edge technology, emerging artists, and innovative ideas.

Austin Food + Wine Festival: For food enthusiasts, the Austin Food + Wine Festival is a culinary delight. Top chefs, restaurants, and wineries come together to showcase their culinary skills and offerings. Attendees can indulge in gourmet tastings, cooking demonstrations, wine pairings, and interactive experiences that celebrate the vibrant food culture of Austin.

Austin Film Festival: This festival celebrates the art and craft of storytelling through film. It features screenings of independent films, panel discussions with filmmakers and industry professionals, scriptwriting competitions, and networking opportunities for aspiring filmmakers and film enthusiasts.

Austin Reggae Festival: Reggae music fans shouldn't miss the Austin Reggae Festival, a three-day event that celebrates reggae music and Jamaican culture. Attendees can enjoy live music performances from local and international reggae artists, delicious Caribbean cuisine, and a laid-back atmosphere perfect for relaxing and soaking in the vibes.

Pecan Street Festival: The Pecan Street Festival is one of the longest-running arts and music festivals in Austin. Held biannually in spring and fall, it features local artisans, craft vendors, live music performances, food trucks, and family-friendly activities. It's a great opportunity to explore Austin's vibrant arts scene and support local artists and businesses.

Austin Urban Music Festival: This festival celebrates the rich diversity of urban music genres, including R&B, hip-hop, soul, and jazz. It features performances by renowned artists, showcases emerging talent, and highlights the influence of urban music on Austin's cultural landscape.

Austin Ice Cream Festival: Beat the heat at the Austin Ice Cream Festival, a fun-filled event that delights ice cream lovers of all ages. Attendees can sample a variety of ice cream flavors from local vendors, participate in ice cream eating contests, enjoy live music, and engage in family-friendly activities.

Austin Powwow and American Indian Heritage Festival: This cultural festival honors Native American heritage and traditions through dance, music, storytelling, arts, and crafts. It's a unique opportunity to learn about indigenous cultures, interact with Native American communities, and celebrate diversity and heritage.

Austin Fermentation Festival: For those interested in fermentation and artisanal food processes, the Austin Fermentation Festival is a must-visit. It showcases fermented foods and beverages from local producers, offers workshops on fermentation techniques, and explores the health benefits of fermented products.

These are just a few highlights of the diverse events and festivals that make Austin a dynamic and exciting destination year-round.

Chapter 11:

Day Trips from Austin

Hill Country wineries

Exploring Hill Country Wineries

Fredericksburg Wine Road 290
Located about an hour and a half west of Austin, Fredericksburg's Wine Road 290 is a must-visit destination for wine enthusiasts. This scenic route is dotted with award-winning wineries, each offering a unique tasting experience. Wineries like Becker Vineyards, Grape Creek Vineyards, and Torre di Pietra Vineyards showcase Texas's winemaking prowess with a variety of wines including robust reds, crisp whites, and refreshing rosés.

Driftwood and Dripping Springs
Head southwest of Austin to discover the charming towns of Driftwood and Dripping Springs, known for their boutique wineries and picturesque settings. Enjoy a leisurely drive through rolling hills adorned with vineyards, stopping at wineries such as Duchman Family Winery, Bell Springs Winery, and Fall Creek Vineyards. Don't miss the opportunity to taste local varietals paired with artisanal cheeses and gourmet bites.

Texas Hill Country Wine Trail

For a comprehensive wine-tasting experience, follow the Texas Hill Country Wine Trail. This trail encompasses numerous wineries across the region, allowing you to sample a diverse range of wines while enjoying the stunning countryside views. Popular stops along the trail include Pedernales Cellars, William Chris Vineyards, and Lost Draw Cellars, where you can learn about the winemaking process and savor handcrafted wines.

Wimberley Valley Wineries

Venture to the quaint town of Wimberley, situated southwest of Austin, to discover hidden gem wineries nestled amidst the tranquil beauty of the Wimberley Valley. Wineries like Driftwood Estate Winery and Wimberley Valley Winery offer a serene wine-tasting experience, often accompanied by live music events or picnics overlooking vineyard landscapes.

Tips for Visiting Hill Country Wineries

Plan Your Route: Map out your winery visits in advance to make the most of your day trip. Consider factors like opening hours, tour availability, and special events.

Designated Driver: If you're planning on indulging in wine tastings, designate a responsible driver or opt for guided tours that provide transportation.

Tasting Fees and Reservations: Some wineries may require reservations for tastings, especially on weekends. Be sure to check their policies and tasting fees beforehand.

Picnic Provisions: Pack a picnic basket with snacks, water, and sunscreen for a relaxing break between tastings. Many wineries have picnic areas where you can enjoy a meal with scenic views.

Explore Beyond Wine: While wine is the highlight, don't overlook other attractions in the area. Explore nearby towns, visit local shops and art galleries, or embark on nature trails for a well-rounded day trip experience.

Respect Winery Etiquette: Follow winery etiquette by avoiding excessive noise, respecting staff and other visitors, and refraining from bringing outside food or drinks unless permitted.

Take Home Souvenirs: Consider purchasing a bottle or two of your favorite wines as souvenirs. Many wineries offer unique varietals that make excellent gifts or mementos of your Hill Country adventure.

San Antonio day trip

San Antonio, located approximately 80 miles southwest of Austin, is renowned for its Spanish colonial heritage, iconic landmarks, and vibrant atmosphere. From the historic Alamo to the scenic River Walk, San Antonio offers a diverse range of attractions that make it an ideal destination for a day trip from Austin.

Getting There

The journey from Austin to San Antonio is conveniently accessible by various modes of transportation, including car, bus, and even train. Interstate 35 South connects the two cities, providing a straightforward and scenic route for travelers. Additionally, several tour companies offer guided day trips from Austin to San Antonio, providing a hassle-free and informative experience.

Top Attractions in San Antonio

The Alamo: A visit to San Antonio is incomplete without exploring the legendary Alamo, a symbol of Texas's struggle for independence. Tour the historic site, learn about the famous Battle of the Alamo, and immerse yourself in Texas history.

San Antonio River Walk: Stroll along the picturesque River Walk, a bustling pedestrian pathway lined with restaurants, shops, and scenic views. Take a boat tour to experience the charm of this iconic waterway.

San Antonio Missions National Historical Park: Discover the UNESCO World Heritage Site comprising four 18th-century Spanish missions, including Mission San Jose and Mission Concepcion. Explore the rich architectural and cultural legacy of these historic sites.

San Antonio Museum of Art: Delve into the world of art and culture at the San Antonio Museum of Art, featuring a diverse collection of artworks spanning centuries and civilizations.

Market Square: Experience the vibrant Mexican culture at Market Square, the largest Mexican market outside of Mexico. Browse through colorful stalls offering authentic crafts, clothing, and culinary delights.

Tower of the Americas: Ascend to the top of the Tower of the Americas for panoramic views of San Antonio skyline and beyond. Enjoy fine dining at the revolving Chart House restaurant or savor a cocktail at the Observation Deck bar.

Historic King William District: Wander through the historic King William District, known for its beautifully preserved Victorian-era homes, art galleries, and charming cafes. Take a guided tour to delve into the district's rich architectural and cultural heritage.

Culinary Delights
San Antonio is a culinary paradise, offering a fusion of Texan, Mexican, and international flavors. Indulge in authentic Tex-Mex cuisine at iconic eateries such as Mi Tierra Café y Panadería or sample gourmet delights at award-winning restaurants along the River Walk.

Shopping and Entertainment
From boutique shops to lively entertainment venues, San Antonio caters to every taste. Explore the eclectic shops at The Shops at La Cantera or enjoy live music and performances at venues like the Aztec Theatre or the Majestic Theatre.

Practical Tips

Plan your day trip in advance to make the most of your time in San Antonio.

Consider purchasing tickets or passes for popular attractions to avoid long queues.

Wear comfortable footwear, especially if you plan to explore the River Walk or historic sites on foot.

Check for any special events or festivals happening in San Antonio during your visit to add to your experience.

Fredericksburg and Enchanted Rock

Fredericksburg

History and Heritage

Fredericksburg's roots trace back to German settlers who arrived in the mid-19th century, leaving a lasting imprint on the town's culture, architecture, and cuisine. Strolling through Fredericksburg's historic district feels like stepping into a European village, with its quaint shops, half-timbered buildings, and welcoming atmosphere.

Main Street Delights

Main Street is the heart of Fredericksburg, offering a delightful mix of boutique shops, art galleries, wine tasting rooms, and restaurants. Visitors can indulge in authentic German fare at eateries like Ausländer Restaurant and Brewery or savor locally sourced dishes at Vaudeville.

Wine and Dine

Fredericksburg's wine scene is renowned, with numerous wineries dotting the surrounding countryside. Wine enthusiasts can embark on a tasting tour along the Texas Wine Trail, discovering award-winning varietals and scenic vineyards. Notable wineries include Becker Vineyards, Grape Creek Vineyards, and Torre di Pietra Vineyards.

Historic Sites
History buffs will appreciate Fredericksburg's historical attractions, such as the National Museum of the Pacific War, dedicated to Admiral Nimitz and World War II in the Pacific. The Pioneer Museum offers insights into early German settlement life, while the Vereins Kirche Museum showcases the town's founding history.

Outdoor Adventures
Nature lovers can explore Fredericksburg's natural beauty at places like Wildseed Farms, a sprawling wildflower farm, or hike along the Fredericksburg Nature Center trails. For a scenic drive, the Willow City Loop offers breathtaking views of wildflowers (seasonal) and rolling hills.

Enchanted Rock

Geological Wonder
A short drive from Fredericksburg lies Enchanted Rock State Natural Area, a geological marvel and a paradise for outdoor enthusiasts. The centerpiece of the park is Enchanted Rock, a massive pink granite dome that rises 425 feet above ground, offering panoramic views of the Texas Hill Country.

Hiking and Rock Climbing

Hikers and climbers flock to Enchanted Rock to conquer its trails and rock formations. The Summit Trail leads to the top of Enchanted Rock, rewarding hikers with sweeping vistas. Rock climbers can test their skills on designated climbing areas, experiencing the thrill of scaling the granite face.

Stargazing and Night Adventures

Enchanted Rock dazzles not only by day but also by night. The park is a designated International Dark Sky Park, making it ideal for stargazing. Visitors can join ranger-led night hikes or simply lay out a blanket for a mesmerizing celestial show.

Picnicking and Relaxation

The park offers ample picnic areas, perfect for a leisurely outdoor meal amidst stunning natural surroundings. Families can enjoy a day of picnicking, wildlife spotting, and exploring the park's diverse ecosystems.

Practical Tips

Getting There: Fredericksburg and Enchanted Rock are approximately 1.5 to 2 hours' drive from Austin, depending on traffic and route chosen.

Best Time to Visit: Spring (March to May) and fall (September to November) offer pleasant weather for outdoor activities and scenic drives.

Accommodations: While day trips are feasible, those wanting a longer stay can find charming bed-and-breakfasts, guesthouses, and inns in Fredericksburg.

Reservations: Enchanted Rock State Natural Area often requires reservations, especially on weekends and holidays, due to its popularity.

Waco and Magnolia Market

Getting There
Waco is conveniently located about 100 miles north of Austin, making it easily accessible by car, bus, or train. The drive typically takes around 1.5 to 2 hours, depending on traffic and route chosen.

Magnolia Market at the Silos
The star attraction in Waco is undoubtedly Magnolia Market at the Silos, founded by Chip and Joanna Gaines, famous for their hit TV show "Fixer Upper." This sprawling complex is a mecca for home decor enthusiasts, offering a unique shopping experience amid a beautifully curated setting. Here's what you can expect:

Shopping: Explore the market's extensive collection of home goods, including furniture, decor items, apparel, and gifts. Whether you're looking for rustic farmhouse charm or modern elegance, Magnolia Market has something for every style.

Silos Baking Co.: Indulge your taste buds at Silos Baking Co., where you can savor freshly baked treats like cupcakes, cookies, and pastries. Don't miss their signature cupcakes, a favorite among visitors.

Food Trucks: Enjoy a variety of culinary delights from the food trucks parked around the Silos. From gourmet sandwiches to refreshing beverages, there's plenty to satisfy your hunger.

Gardens and Play Area: Take a leisurely stroll through the lush gardens surrounding the Silos, perfect for a relaxing break. Families with children can also enjoy the spacious play area, complete with swings and climbing structures.

Events and Workshops: Check the calendar for special events, workshops, and live music performances hosted at Magnolia Market throughout the year. It's a great way to immerse yourself in the local culture and creativity.

Other Attractions in Waco

While Magnolia Market is a highlight, Waco offers more to explore beyond the Silos:

Waco Mammoth National Monument: Uncover the prehistoric past at this fascinating site, where mammoth fossils are on display. Guided tours provide insights into paleontology and the history of these ancient giants.

Cameron Park Zoo: Ideal for families, Cameron Park Zoo is home to a diverse array of wildlife, including lions, elephants, and tropical birds. Interactive exhibits and educational programs make it both entertaining and educational.

Dr Pepper Museum: Dive into soda history at the Dr Pepper Museum, located in a historic building downtown. Learn about the origins of Dr Pepper and explore exhibits showcasing vintage bottling equipment and memorabilia.

Texas Ranger Hall of Fame and Museum: Discover the storied legacy of the Texas Rangers, renowned law enforcement figures in the state's history. The museum exhibits artifacts, weapons, and tales of frontier justice.

Tips for Your Day Trip

Plan Ahead: Check the opening hours and any special events at Magnolia Market to make the most of your visit.

Comfortable Attire: Wear comfortable shoes and clothing, especially if you plan to explore the outdoor areas or shop extensively.

Bring a Camera: Capture the charm of Magnolia Market and your adventures in Waco with a camera or smartphone. The picturesque settings are perfect for memorable photos.

Try Local Eateries: Venture beyond the tourist spots and sample some of Waco's local restaurants for a taste of authentic Texas cuisine.

Respectful Exploration: When visiting cultural or historical sites, observe any guidelines or rules to ensure a respectful and enjoyable experience for everyone.

Enchanted Rock State Natural Area

Located just about 90 minutes from Austin, Enchanted Rock State Natural Area is a captivating destination for outdoor enthusiasts and nature lovers. This iconic geological marvel offers a range of activities, from hiking and rock climbing to stargazing and picnicking, making it a must-visit day trip from Austin.

Getting There The journey from Austin to Enchanted Rock is part of the adventure. Take US-290 W and then turn onto Ranch Road 965, leading you to the park's entrance. The drive itself is scenic, passing through the picturesque Texas Hill Country, known for its rolling hills and charming landscapes.

Overview of Enchanted Rock Enchanted Rock is a massive pink granite dome that rises 425 feet above ground, making it one of the largest batholiths (underground rock formations exposed by erosion) in the United States. It holds both geological and cultural significance, with Native American legends adding to its allure.

Activities

Hiking: The park offers several trails catering to different skill levels. The Summit Trail is the most popular, leading hikers to the top of Enchanted Rock for breathtaking panoramic views of the surrounding area. Other trails include the Loop Trail and the Echo Canyon Trail, each showcasing unique aspects of the park's natural beauty.

Rock Climbing: Enchanted Rock is a hotspot for rock climbers, with numerous routes ranging from beginner-friendly to challenging. Visitors can enjoy the thrill of scaling the granite walls under the vast Texas sky.

Stargazing: As evening falls, Enchanted Rock transforms into a prime stargazing spot. Away from city lights, the night sky here is a spectacle, perfect for astronomy enthusiasts or anyone seeking a peaceful night under the stars.

Picnicking: The park provides designated picnic areas where visitors can relax and enjoy a meal amidst stunning rock formations and scenic landscapes. It's an ideal way to unwind and connect with nature.

Tips for Visiting

Reservations: Due to its popularity, especially on weekends and holidays, it's advisable to make reservations in advance, especially if you plan to camp or visit during peak seasons.

Comfortable Clothing and Footwear: Whether you're hiking or climbing, wear comfortable clothing and sturdy footwear suitable for outdoor activities.

Water and Snacks: Carry an ample supply of water and snacks, especially if you're planning an extended stay or engaging in strenuous activities.

Sun Protection: The Texas sun can be intense, so don't forget sunscreen, hats, and sunglasses to protect yourself from UV rays.

Leave No Trace: Respect the natural environment by following Leave No Trace principles, ensuring you leave the park as pristine as you found it.

Nearby Attractions While Enchanted Rock is the highlight of this day trip, there are other attractions worth exploring nearby:

Fredericksburg: A charming town known for its German heritage, wineries, and boutiques. Take some time to wander through its historic streets and enjoy local cuisine and shopping.

Luckenbach: A tiny, iconic Texas town famous for its live music scene and laid-back atmosphere. It's a great place to unwind and soak in the Texas Hill Country vibe.

Wildseed Farms: Located in Fredericksburg, this expansive wildflower farm offers scenic beauty, shopping for garden enthusiasts, and a chance to experience Texas flora up close.

Chapter 12:

Practical Tips for Visitors

Weather and what to pack

Understanding Austin's Weather

Seasonal Variations

Summer (June to August): Summers in Austin are hot and humid, with temperatures often reaching the high 90s°F (35-38°C). Be prepared for intense sunlight and occasional thunderstorms, especially in the afternoons.

Fall (September to November): Fall brings relief from the summer heat, with temperatures ranging from the mid-60s°F to mid-80s°F (18-30°C). It's a pleasant time to visit, although occasional rain showers are possible.

Winter (December to February): Winters in Austin are mild, with daytime temperatures averaging in the 50s°F (10-15°C). However, nights can get chilly, dropping into the 30s°F (1-4°C). Snow is rare but not unheard of.

Spring (March to May): Spring is a beautiful time in Austin, with temperatures rising from the 60s°F to 80s°F (15-30°C). It's a popular season for outdoor activities and festivals.

Humidity and Rainfall
Austin experiences moderate humidity, especially in the summer months, which can make the heat feel more intense.
Rainfall is spread fairly evenly throughout the year, but the wettest months are typically May and October. Pack accordingly for possible rain showers.

Sun Protection
Given Austin's sunny weather, sun protection is crucial. Pack sunscreen with a high SPF, sunglasses, a wide-brimmed hat, and lightweight, breathable clothing to stay cool.

What to Pack

Clothing

Summer: Light and breathable fabrics like cotton or moisture-wicking materials are ideal. Shorts, T-shirts, sundresses, and sandals are perfect for daytime outings. Don't forget a swimsuit if you plan to visit water attractions
Fall: Bring layers such as light sweaters, long-sleeve shirts, and jeans for cooler evenings. A light jacket or hoodie may be needed.

Winter: While winters are mild, pack a mix of long-sleeve shirts, sweaters, jeans, and a heavier jacket or coat for colder nights. A scarf and gloves can be handy, especially if you plan outdoor activities.

Spring: Similar to fall, pack layers for varying temperatures. Light jackets or cardigans, along with T-shirts and jeans, work well.

Footwear
Comfortable walking shoes are essential, especially if you plan to explore Austin's outdoor attractions like parks and trails. Sneakers, sandals, or hiking shoes are suitable choices.

Accessories
In addition to sun protection items, consider packing a reusable water bottle to stay hydrated, a daypack for carrying essentials during outings, and a portable umbrella or rain jacket for unexpected showers.

Technology and Gadgets
Don't forget to bring chargers for your devices, a power bank for on-the-go charging, and any necessary adapters if you're traveling from outside the U.S.

Medical and Personal Items
Pack any prescription medications, along with a basic first aid kit for minor emergencies. Include insect repellent, especially if you plan outdoor activities in wooded areas.

Travel Documents
Ensure you have your passport (if international), ID, travel insurance information, accommodation details, and any tickets or reservations printed or accessible electronically.

Additional Tips

Stay Hydrated: Drink plenty of water, especially during hot summer days, to avoid dehydration.

Plan for Outdoor Activities: If you're visiting parks or participating in outdoor sports, pack appropriate gear like a picnic blanket, sports equipment, or binoculars for birdwatching.

Local Cuisine: Austin is known for its diverse culinary scene. Pack an appetite to explore Tex-Mex dishes, BBQ joints, food trucks, and craft breweries.

Respect Local Customs: Familiarize yourself with Austin's culture and etiquette, such as tipping practices and respecting personal space in crowded areas.

Safety tips

Stay Informed: Before your trip, familiarize yourself with the areas you plan to visit. Know the neighborhoods, attractions, and any potential safety concerns specific to those areas.

Use Reputable Accommodations: Choose hotels or accommodations with good reviews and in safe neighborhoods. Consider factors like proximity to public transportation and well-lit areas.

Keep Valuables Secure: While exploring the city, keep your valuables such as wallets, phones, and passports secure. Use a money belt or secure pockets to deter pickpockets.

Be Cautious at Night: Avoid walking alone in unfamiliar or dimly lit areas, especially at night. Stick to well-lit streets and populated areas. If you plan to enjoy Austin's nightlife, arrange for transportation in advance or use reputable rideshare services.

Stay Alert in Crowded Places: Austin's popular attractions and events can draw large crowds. Stay vigilant in crowded areas, watch out for pickpockets, and keep your belongings close.

Follow Traffic Laws: If you're driving in Austin, obey traffic laws, wear your seatbelt, and avoid distracted driving. Be mindful of cyclists and pedestrians, especially in downtown areas.

Stay Hydrated: Austin's climate can be hot, especially in the summer months. Stay hydrated by drinking plenty of water, especially if you're outdoors or participating in outdoor activities.

Know Emergency Numbers: Familiarize yourself with emergency numbers such as 911 for immediate assistance. Save important contacts like your hotel, local police, and embassy or consulate if you're an international visitor.

Use Caution with Alcohol: If you choose to drink alcohol, do so responsibly. Pace yourself, know your limits, and avoid excessive drinking, which can impair judgment and make you vulnerable.

Respect Local Laws and Customs: Familiarize yourself with local laws, customs, and cultural norms. Be respectful of local residents, traditions, and public spaces.

Stay Informed About Weather: Austin can experience rapid weather changes, including thunderstorms and heatwaves. Stay informed about weather forecasts and take precautions accordingly.

Use Common Sense: Trust your instincts and use common sense in unfamiliar situations. If something feels unsafe or uncomfortable, remove yourself from the situation and seek assistance if needed.

Local etiquette and customs

Southern Hospitality: Texans are known for their warm hospitality and friendly demeanor. It's common to greet people with a smile and engage in polite conversation, even with strangers. Don't be surprised if locals strike up a conversation while waiting in line or sitting at a cafe.

Respect for Diversity: Austin prides itself on its diversity and inclusivity. Respect for different cultures, beliefs, and lifestyles is highly valued. Avoid making assumptions or stereotyping people based on appearance or background.

Texan Politeness: "Yes, ma'am" and "Yes, sir" are common expressions of politeness in Texas, regardless of age. Using these terms when addressing locals, especially elders, shows respect and courtesy.

Punctuality: Texans generally appreciate punctuality. Whether you're attending a business meeting, a social gathering, or a cultural event, arriving on time or slightly early is considered respectful.

Dress Code: Austin's dress code is often casual and laid-back, reflecting its vibrant and eclectic culture. However, for certain occasions like fine dining restaurants or formal events, smart casual attire is appropriate. Always check the dress code if you're unsure.

Tipping Culture: Tipping is customary in Austin, especially in restaurants, bars, and for services like taxi rides or haircuts. A standard tip for good service is around 15-20% of the total bill. Be mindful of this practice to show appreciation for excellent service.

Public Behavior: Austin promotes a relaxed and open-minded atmosphere, but public behavior should still be respectful and considerate. Avoid loud or disruptive behavior in public spaces, and be mindful of others' comfort.

Environmental Awareness: Texans are increasingly conscious of environmental issues. Participate in eco-friendly practices such as recycling, conserving water, and supporting businesses that prioritize sustainability.

Traffic and Transportation: Austin's traffic can be busy, especially during peak hours. Plan your travel accordingly, and consider using alternative transportation like public buses, rideshare services, or biking to navigate the city more efficiently.

Alcohol Consumption: While Austin has a vibrant nightlife and a thriving bar scene, it's important to drink responsibly. Public intoxication is not tolerated, and designated drivers or rideshare services are encouraged for safe transportation after drinking.

Cultural Sensitivity: Austin is home to a rich tapestry of cultures, including Native American, Hispanic, African American, and various immigrant communities. Show respect for cultural traditions, customs, and heritage sites you visit.

Language: English is the primary language spoken in Austin, but you may encounter Spanish speakers and other languages due to the city's diverse population. Learning a few basic phrases in Spanish can be helpful and appreciated.

Outdoor Etiquette: Austin's natural beauty and outdoor spaces are treasured by locals and visitors alike. Follow trail etiquettes, such as staying on designated paths, cleaning up after picnics or hikes, and respecting wildlife and nature conservation efforts.

Shopping and Bargaining: While bargaining is not common in most retail stores, it's acceptable in some markets and flea markets. Use your judgment and be respectful when negotiating prices.

Emergency Preparedness: Familiarize yourself with emergency contacts, including local police, fire departments, hospitals, and embassy or consulate information if you're an international visitor. It's always wise to have a basic understanding of local emergency procedures.

Currency and payment methods

Understanding the currency and payment methods is essential for any traveler visiting Austin, Texas. Here's everything you need to know to manage your finances effectively during your trip.

Currency: The official currency of the United States is the US Dollar ($). Notes come in denominations of $1, $5, $10, $20, $50, and $100. Coins are also used, including pennies (1 cent), nickels (5 cents), dimes (10 cents), and quarters (25 cents).

Exchange Rates: Before your trip, it's advisable to check the exchange rates to have an idea of how much your home currency is worth in US Dollars. You can do this through banks, currency exchange offices, or online currency converters.

Currency Exchange: Austin has several currency exchange offices and banks where you can exchange your money. Major airports, such as Austin-Bergstrom International Airport, also have currency exchange services. However, keep in mind that exchange rates at airports may not be as favorable as those in the city.

ATMs: ATMs are widely available throughout Austin, especially in popular tourist areas, hotels, and shopping centers. Most ATMs accept international cards with major networks like Visa, Mastercard, American Express, and Discover. However, it's advisable to inform your bank about your travel plans to avoid any issues with card usage abroad.

Credit Cards: Credit cards are widely accepted in Austin, including Visa, Mastercard, American Express, and Discover. You can use your credit card for various transactions, including shopping, dining, and entertainment. It's a convenient and secure way to make payments, but be aware of any foreign transaction fees that your card issuer may apply.

Debit Cards: Debit cards linked to major networks like Visa or Mastercard are also accepted at most establishments in Austin. They can be used to withdraw cash from ATMs and make purchases. Like credit cards, check with your bank regarding international usage fees and ATM withdrawal limits.

Traveler's Checks: Although traveler's checks are less commonly used today, some places in Austin may still accept them. However, they are not as convenient as credit or debit cards, and you may encounter difficulties in finding places that will cash them.

Mobile Payments: Mobile payment options like Apple Pay, Google Pay, and Samsung Pay are gaining popularity in Austin. Many retailers, restaurants, and even public transportation systems accept mobile payments, providing a convenient and contactless way to pay for your purchases.

Tips for Managing Your Finances
Notify your bank and credit card companies about your travel dates and destinations to prevent any blocks on your cards due to suspicious activity.
Keep a record of important numbers, such as your bank's customer service hotline and your card's emergency contact number, in case of lost or stolen cards.
Use ATMs located in well-lit and secure areas, especially at night, to ensure your safety.
Monitor your bank statements and transactions regularly to detect any unauthorized charges promptly.
Carry a mix of payment methods, including cash, credit cards, and a backup debit card, for flexibility and security.

Essential Phrases

When visiting Austin, Texas, knowing some essential phrases can enhance your experience and make interactions smoother. While English is widely spoken, Austin's unique cultural blend sometimes introduces regional phrases and expressions that can add charm to your conversations. Here are some essential phrases to help you navigate your trip:

"Howdy!" - This traditional Texan greeting is friendly and welcoming, often used in casual settings.

"Y'all" - A contraction of "you all," commonly used in Southern dialects to address a group of people.

"Hook 'em Horns!" - The rallying cry of the University of Texas at Austin, often used by locals to show support for the Longhorns.

"Keep Austin Weird" - A slogan embraced by Austinites, celebrating the city's quirky and unique culture.

"Bless your heart" - A Southern expression that can convey sympathy, understanding, or even a subtle form of criticism depending on the context.

"Texas-sized" - Refers to something large or extravagant, highlighting Texas's penchant for grandeur.

"Fixin' to" - Means getting ready to do something soon, a common phrase in Southern speech.

"How's it goin'?" - A casual way to ask someone how they are doing.

"Can I get a refill?" - Useful when dining out to request more of a beverage.

"Where's the nearest BBQ joint?" - Because no visit to Austin is complete without indulging in some delicious barbecue.

"I'll have a Shiner Bock, please" - Ordering a popular Texan beer often enjoyed with meals.

"How do I get to Barton Springs Pool?" - A must-visit natural spring pool in Austin.

"What's the live music scene like tonight?" - Austin's renowned live music scene is a major attraction for visitors.

"Do you have any vegetarian options?" - Useful for those with dietary preferences or restrictions.

"Thank y'all kindly!" - A gracious way to express gratitude, combining "thank you" with the Southern flair of "y'all."

Additional Practical Tips for Visitors

Weather and Clothing: Austin experiences hot summers and mild winters. Pack lightweight clothing for summer visits and layer up for cooler months. Don't forget a hat, sunglasses, and sunscreen, especially if you plan outdoor activities.

Transportation: Consider renting a car for convenience, as Austin's attractions are spread out. Ride-hailing services and public transit are also available.

Currency and Payments: U.S. dollars are widely accepted. Credit and debit cards are preferred for transactions, but it's always good to have some cash on hand for smaller purchases and tips.

Local Etiquette: Texans are known for their friendliness. It's customary to greet people with a smile and a nod, and holding doors open for others is appreciated.

Safety: Austin is generally safe, but it's wise to stay aware of your surroundings, especially in crowded areas or at night. Keep valuables secure and be cautious when exploring unfamiliar neighborhoods.

Tap Water: Austin's tap water is safe to drink and often preferred by locals. Carry a reusable water bottle to stay hydrated, especially during outdoor activities.

Emergency Numbers: Know the emergency numbers for Austin, including 911 for emergencies and local police/fire department contacts.

Healthcare: Familiarize yourself with nearby medical facilities and pharmacies in case of any health concerns during your trip.

Respect Local Culture: Embrace Austin's diverse and inclusive culture. Be respectful of different lifestyles, traditions, and beliefs you encounter during your visit.

Stay Updated: Check local news and weather updates for any changes or events that may impact your plans.

Useful Contacts (Emergency Numbers, Tourism Offices)

Emergency Numbers

911: This is the universal emergency number in the United States for immediate assistance from police, fire, or medical services in life-threatening situations.

Austin Police Department (Non-Emergency): For non-emergency situations requiring police assistance or reporting incidents, you can contact the Austin Police Department at [Non-Emergency Number].

Austin Fire Department (Non-Emergency): For non-emergency fire-related concerns or inquiries, reach out to the Austin Fire Department at [Non-Emergency Number].

Austin-Travis County Emergency Medical Services (EMS): For medical emergencies and ambulance services, contact Austin-Travis County EMS at [Emergency Medical Services Number].

Tourism Offices

Austin Convention and Visitors Bureau (Visit Austin): The official tourism office of Austin, Visit Austin provides comprehensive information on attractions, events, accommodations, dining, and more. Contact them at [Visit Austin Contact Information] or visit their website at [Visit Austin Website].

Texas Department of Transportation (TXDOT): For road conditions, traffic updates, and travel advisories in and around

Austin, TXDOT offers real-time information. Visit their website at [TXDOT Website] or contact them at [TXDOT Contact Information].

Austin-Bergstrom International Airport (ABIA): If you need information regarding flights, airport facilities, transportation options, or general inquiries about ABIA, contact the airport directly at [ABIA Contact Information].

Austin Visitor Center: Located in the heart of downtown Austin, the Visitor Center offers maps, brochures, guides, and personalized assistance for tourists. Contact them at [Visitor Center Contact Information] or visit them at [Visitor Center Address].

Additional Tips for Visitors

Weather and What to Pack: Austin experiences a diverse climate, with hot summers and mild winters. Pack lightweight clothing for summer visits and layer up during cooler months. Don't forget sunscreen, a hat, and sunglasses for sun protection.

Local Etiquette and Customs: Austin embraces a casual and friendly atmosphere. Respect local customs, such as saying "y'all" (short for "you all") and being courteous on public transportation or in crowded areas.

Currency and Payment Methods: The official currency in Austin is the US Dollar (USD). Credit and debit cards are widely accepted, but it's advisable to carry some cash for small purchases and transactions.

Essential Phrases for Travelers: While English is the primary language spoken in Austin, knowing a few basic phrases can be helpful:

"Howdy!" - A friendly greeting often used in Texas.
"Where is the nearest [restaurant/hotel/bathroom]?" - Useful for navigation.
"Thank you" - A simple gesture of appreciation.
"Can I have the check, please?" - When dining out or making payments.

Chapter 13:

Family-Friendly Activities

Theme Parks and Zoos

Theme Parks

Austin's Park and Pizza: This expansive entertainment center is a paradise for families. With thrilling rides like go-karts, bumper boats, and mini-golf, it promises hours of excitement. The park also features an arcade, batting cages, and a pizza buffet, making it a one-stop destination for fun and food.

Kiddie Acres: Perfect for younger children, Kiddie Acres offers a nostalgic carnival experience with classic rides like carousels, mini trains, and a Ferris wheel. Families can enjoy a relaxed atmosphere and create lasting memories with their little ones.

ZDT's Amusement Park: Although located slightly outside Austin in Seguin, ZDT's Amusement Park is worth the trip. It combines thrilling rides like the Switchback roller coaster with water attractions like the Torrent River for a day of adventure and cool splashes.

Zoos and Animal Encounters

Austin Zoo: Unlike traditional zoos, the Austin Zoo focuses on rescuing and rehabilitating animals. Visitors can see a diverse range of rescued animals, including big cats, primates, and exotic birds. Educational programs and feeding sessions add to the experience, making it both entertaining and informative.

Capital of Texas Zoo: Located in Bastrop, just a short drive from Austin, this zoo offers a more intimate setting with a variety of animals from around the world. Highlights include the Lemur Island, where lemurs roam freely, and interactive experiences like feeding giraffes and petting zoos for younger visitors.

SeaWorld San Antonio: While not in Austin, SeaWorld San Antonio is a must-visit for families seeking marine adventures. From captivating shows featuring dolphins and orcas to thrilling rides like the Steel Eel roller coaster, SeaWorld offers a blend of entertainment and education about marine life conservation.

Tips for Enjoying Family-Friendly Activities

Plan Ahead: Check operating hours and any special events or shows at theme parks and zoos before your visit. Planning ahead ensures you don't miss out on any highlights.

Pack Essentials: Bring sunscreen, hats, and comfortable clothing for outdoor activities. Snacks and water bottles are also handy, especially for full days of exploration.

Take Breaks: Pace your day to avoid exhaustion, especially if visiting multiple attractions. Plan breaks for snacks or quiet moments to recharge.

Capture Memories: Bring a camera or smartphone to capture memorable moments with family members and the fascinating animals or thrilling rides you encounter.

Respect Wildlife: When interacting with animals, follow guidelines provided by zoo staff for your safety and the well-being of the animals. Avoid feeding animals unless it's part of a supervised experience.

Check for Discounts: Many theme parks and zoos offer discounts for families, especially if you book tickets online or look for promotional deals.

Educational Centers

The Thinkery
Located in the Mueller neighborhood, The Thinkery is a hands-on children's museum that sparks curiosity and creativity through interactive exhibits and programs. It's a perfect blend of science, technology, engineering, art, and math (STEAM) for kids of all ages. The museum features areas like the Innovators' Workshop, where kids can engage in tinkering and building projects, and the Kitchen Lab, where they can explore the science of cooking.

Austin Nature & Science Center

Nestled in the Zilker Park area, the Austin Nature & Science Center offers a fascinating journey into the natural world and scientific exploration. Families can enjoy wildlife exhibits, nature trails, and interactive programs focusing on geology, paleontology, and wildlife conservation. The Dino Pit is a highlight, allowing kids to uncover and learn about fossils like real paleontologists.

Bullock Texas State History Museum
For a deep dive into Texas history, the Bullock Texas State History Museum is a must-visit. Located near the State Capitol, this museum showcases the rich cultural heritage of Texas through immersive exhibits, artifacts, and multimedia presentations. Families can explore topics ranging from Native American history to the Texas Revolution and modern-day cultural contributions.

Austin Zoo & Animal Sanctuary
While not a traditional educational center, the Austin Zoo offers a unique learning experience about wildlife conservation and animal welfare. It's home to rescued and rehabilitated animals, providing an up-close look at species from around the world. Educational programs and guided tours enhance the experience, highlighting the importance of environmental stewardship.

Lady Bird Johnson Wildflower Center
Nature lovers and budding botanists will delight in the Lady Bird Johnson Wildflower Center. This botanical garden and research center focus on native plants, conservation, and sustainable landscaping. Families can explore gardens filled with Texas

wildflowers, attend educational workshops, and learn about ecological stewardship practices.

Science Mill
A short drive from Austin in Johnson City, the Science Mill offers a blend of science and technology in a historic mill setting. Interactive exhibits cover a wide range of topics such as robotics, renewable energy, and nanotechnology. Hands-on activities and demonstrations engage visitors of all ages in the wonders of STEM fields.

Texas Memorial Museum
Located on the University of Texas at Austin campus, the Texas Memorial Museum is a treasure trove of natural history. Families can explore exhibits on paleontology, geology, biology, and Texas wildlife. The highlight is the Hall of Geology and Paleontology, featuring dinosaur skeletons and fossils that fascinate both kids and adults.

Austin Aquarium
While primarily an entertainment venue, the Austin Aquarium also provides educational experiences about marine life and conservation. Families can observe diverse aquatic species, participate in feeding sessions, and learn about ocean ecosystems. Educational talks and interactive touch tanks offer insights into marine biology and environmental conservation efforts.

Tips for Visiting Educational Centers with Family

Plan Ahead: Check the opening hours, ticket prices, and any special events or exhibits before your visit.

Interactive Participation: Encourage kids to actively engage with exhibits through hands-on activities and guided programs.

Learning Opportunities: Take advantage of educational workshops, demonstrations, and talks offered by the centers.

Pack Essentials: Carry water bottles, snacks, sunscreen, and comfortable walking shoes for a day of exploration.

Capture Memories: Bring a camera or smartphone to capture memorable moments and discoveries during your visit.

Playgrounds and Picnic Areas

Playgrounds

Zilker Park Playground: Located in the heart of Austin, Zilker Park offers one of the most iconic playgrounds in the city. Kids can climb, swing, and slide amidst the beautiful backdrop of Zilker Park's greenery. The playground is designed with various age-appropriate structures, ensuring that children of all ages can have a great time.

Mueller Lake Park: This expansive park in the Mueller community features a modern playground with innovative equipment. From climbing walls to interactive play structures, Mueller Lake Park offers a diverse range of activities for kids.

The nearby lake adds to the scenic charm, making it a perfect spot for a family outing.

Dick Nichols District Park: Nestled in Southwest Austin, Dick Nichols District Park boasts a large playground area with ample space for kids to run and play. The park's shady trees and picnic tables make it ideal for a day of outdoor fun and relaxation.

Pease Park: Known for its natural beauty and historic significance, Pease Park also offers a playground area that blends seamlessly into the park's landscape. Children can enjoy play structures while parents appreciate the park's serene ambiance and picnic spots nearby.

Butler Park: Situated near downtown Austin, Butler Park features a playground with a splash pad, perfect for hot summer days. Families can combine playtime with water fun, making it a refreshing choice for a family outing.

Picnic Areas

Barton Springs Picnic Area: Adjacent to Barton Springs Pool, this picnic area provides a scenic view of the springs and ample space for picnics. Families can enjoy a meal surrounded by nature before or after a swim in the iconic Barton Springs Pool.

Mayfield Park and Preserve: Known for its peacocks and tranquil gardens, Mayfield Park also offers picnic tables amidst lush greenery. It's a peaceful retreat within the city, ideal for a relaxed family picnic.

Emma Long Metropolitan Park: For families looking for a lakeside picnic experience, Emma Long Park delivers with its picturesque setting along Lake Austin. The park's amenities include picnic tables, BBQ pits, and opportunities for water activities, making it a full-day destination for families.

Commons Ford Ranch Metropolitan Park: This spacious park along Lake Austin features multiple picnic areas with stunning waterfront views. Families can enjoy picnicking, hiking trails, and birdwatching, immersing themselves in Austin's natural beauty.

Brushy Creek Lake Park: While technically located in Cedar Park, Brushy Creek Lake Park is worth the short drive for its scenic picnic spots and playgrounds. Families can enjoy lakeside picnics, fishing, and exploring the park's trails and wildlife.

Family-Friendly Attractions

Austin Nature & Science Center: Perfect for a blend of education and fun, the Austin Nature & Science Center offers interactive exhibits, nature trails, and wildlife encounters. It's a great way for kids to learn about the natural world while having hands-on experiences.

Thinkery: Located in Mueller, Thinkery is a children's museum that sparks creativity and curiosity through interactive exhibits and workshops. From science to art and technology, Thinkery offers engaging activities for kids of all ages.

Austin Zoo: Home to a variety of rescued animals, the Austin Zoo provides a unique opportunity for families to see wildlife up close. The zoo's focus on education and conservation makes it both entertaining and educational for visitors.

The Bullock Texas State History Museum: While history might not always be the first choice for kids, the Bullock Museum offers engaging exhibits and programs that bring Texas history to life. It's a chance for families to delve into the state's rich heritage together.

Austin Aquarium: For families interested in marine life, the Austin Aquarium features a diverse range of exhibits, including interactive touch tanks and opportunities to feed animals. It's a hands-on experience that appeals to both kids and adults.

Chapter 14:

Insider's Tips

Hidden Gems in Austin

Mayfield Park and Preserve: Tucked away from the city's hustle, Mayfield Park offers a serene escape with its lush gardens and resident peacocks. Take a leisurely stroll through the gardens, enjoy a picnic by the ponds, and marvel at the historic cottage, all while surrounded by beautiful flora and fauna.

Mount Bonnell at Sunset: For panoramic views of the Colorado River and the Austin skyline, head to Mount Bonnell, especially during sunset. The short hike up the stairs rewards you with breathtaking vistas, making it an ideal spot for romantic moments or peaceful contemplation.

Graffiti Park at Castle Hill: Street art enthusiasts will find paradise at Graffiti Park, officially known as the HOPE Outdoor Gallery. This ever-changing outdoor gallery showcases colorful graffiti and murals, offering a dynamic and vibrant urban art experience.

The Cathedral of Junk: A quirky and unique attraction, the Cathedral of Junk is an art installation made entirely of discarded items like bicycles, toys, and metal scraps. Explore this whimsical creation, interact with the artist behind it, and marvel at the creativity that transforms junk into art.

Barton Springs After Dark: While Barton Springs Pool is a popular destination for cooling off during the day, experiencing it after dark is a whole new adventure. During certain times of the year, you can enjoy night swims under the stars, accompanied by live music and a magical ambiance.

The Moonlight Towers: Austin is home to a few remaining Moonlight Towers, historic lighting fixtures dating back to the late 19th century. Take a nighttime stroll near these towers in neighborhoods like Zilker or West Campus to witness their nostalgic glow and learn about their fascinating history.

Hamilton Pool Preserve: A natural oasis located just outside Austin, Hamilton Pool Preserve boasts a stunning collapsed grotto and emerald-green waters. Reserve your spot in advance to swim in this picturesque setting surrounded by towering cliffs and lush vegetation.

The Contemporary Austin - Laguna Gloria: Art and nature converge seamlessly at Laguna Gloria, a sculpture garden and museum overlooking Lake Austin. Explore outdoor art installations, stroll through manicured gardens, and immerse yourself in the beauty of this cultural gem.

Chicken Shit Bingo at Ginny's Little Longhorn Saloon: Experience a quirky Texan tradition at Ginny's Little Longhorn Saloon with Chicken Shit Bingo. Yes, you read that right! Watch as chickens roam on a numbered grid, placing their bets on where they'll do their business, creating a hilarious and unique form of entertainment.

Lady Bird Lake Boardwalk at Sunrise: Start your day with a tranquil walk or bike ride along the Lady Bird Lake Boardwalk during sunrise. Witness the city awaken as the sun paints the sky in hues of gold and pink, casting a magical glow over the water and surrounding skyline.

Elisabet Ney Museum: Delve into Austin's artistic heritage at the Elisabet Ney Museum, dedicated to the renowned sculptor. Explore Ney's studio and gardens, admire her sculptures, and gain insight into the city's cultural evolution through the eyes of this pioneering artist.

Secret Beach on the Colorado River: Escape the crowds and discover Austin's Secret Beach, a hidden spot along the Colorado River. Accessible via a short hike, this secluded beach offers a peaceful retreat for swimming, sunbathing, and enjoying the natural beauty of the riverbanks.

East Austin Studio Tour (EAST): If you're visiting Austin in November, don't miss the East Austin Studio Tour, an annual event where local artists open their studios to the public. Explore diverse artworks, meet artists, and get a glimpse into Austin's thriving art scene.

Hike to Sculpture Falls: For a refreshing outdoor adventure, embark on a hike to Sculpture Falls in the Barton Creek Greenbelt. Follow the trails lined with scenic views, and reward yourself with a dip in the natural swimming hole surrounded by lush greenery.

Explore Historic East Sixth Street: While Sixth Street is famous for its nightlife, delve deeper into Historic East Sixth Street during the day. Discover eclectic shops, cozy cafes, art galleries, and hidden gems that showcase Austin's vibrant cultural tapestry beyond its nocturnal reputation.

Budget-Friendly Activities

Explore the Green Spaces
Austin is blessed with beautiful parks and green spaces, perfect for a budget-friendly day out. Zilker Park, the city's crown jewel, offers free access and a range of activities. Take a leisurely stroll along Lady Bird Lake, have a picnic with stunning skyline views, or join a free yoga session in the park.

Visit Barton Springs Pool
While some attractions in Austin come with a price tag, Barton Springs Pool is an affordable gem. Located within Zilker Park, this natural spring-fed pool offers a refreshing escape during hot Texas days. Admission fees are modest, especially considering the unique experience it offers.

Enjoy Live Music
Austin's reputation as the Live Music Capital of the World doesn't mean you have to spend a lot to enjoy great tunes. Many bars and venues offer free live music nights, especially during weekdays. Check out places like The Continental Club,

Elephant Room, or Spider House Cafe for budget-friendly music experiences.

Explore Street Art and Murals
Austin's streets are adorned with colorful murals and street art, making it a paradise for art enthusiasts and Instagrammers. Take a self-guided walking tour of the city's most famous murals, such as the "Greetings from Austin" mural on South First Street or the "I Love You So Much" wall on South Congress Avenue.

Visit Museums on Free Days
Several museums in Austin offer free admission days or evenings, allowing you to explore art, history, and culture without spending a dime. The Blanton Museum of Art, Bullock Texas State History Museum, and the Contemporary Austin are just a few that offer free entry on specific days.

Attend Free Events and Festivals
Austin is known for its vibrant festival scene, and many of these events offer free entry to certain parts or days. Keep an eye out for events like SXSW (South by Southwest) with free outdoor concerts, Austin City Limits Music Festival's free aftershows, or the Pecan Street Festival for arts, crafts, and live music.

Explore Food Trucks
Austin's food truck culture is not only delicious but also budget-friendly. From gourmet tacos to mouthwatering BBQ, you can sample a variety of cuisines without splurging. Head to food truck parks like The Picnic or South Congress Avenue for a culinary adventure on a budget.

Hike and Bike Trails

Get active and explore Austin's natural beauty by hiking or biking along its scenic trails. The Ann and Roy Butler Hike-and-Bike Trail along Lady Bird Lake offers picturesque views of the city skyline and is free for all to enjoy. Bring your own bike or rent one from one of the city's bike-sharing services.

Explore Historic Neighborhoods

Take a stroll through Austin's historic neighborhoods like Hyde Park, East Cesar Chavez, or Bouldin Creek. Admire the architecture, browse local shops, and soak in the laid-back atmosphere without spending a dime.

Attend Free Yoga and Fitness Classes

Many studios and fitness centers in Austin offer free or donation-based yoga and fitness classes, especially during community events or promotional periods. Check out local listings or social media pages for upcoming free classes and wellness activities.

Visit Farmer's Markets

Experience Austin's local flavors and support small businesses by visiting farmer's markets like the Sustainable Food Center's Downtown Farmers' Market or the Texas Farmers' Market at Mueller. Sample fresh produce, artisanal goods, and enjoy a vibrant market atmosphere without spending much.

Take a Self-Guided Brewery Tour

While formal brewery tours may come with a price, you can create your own self-guided tour of Austin's craft breweries.

Many breweries offer free tastings or affordable flights, allowing you to sample a variety of local brews without breaking your budget.

Explore University Campuses
Austin is home to prestigious universities like the University of Texas at Austin. Take a self-guided tour of the campuses, admire the architecture, visit libraries and museums, and soak in the academic atmosphere for free.

Attend Free Workshops and Classes
Keep an eye out for free workshops, classes, and lectures offered by local businesses, libraries, and community centers. From art workshops to cooking classes and tech seminars, there's always something interesting to learn without spending money.

Enjoy Sunset Views
Witness breathtaking sunsets without spending a dime by heading to spots like Mount Bonnell, Pennybacker Bridge (360 Bridge), or the Boardwalk at Lady Bird Lake. Pack a picnic, relax, and enjoy nature's beauty as the sun sets over Austin.

Sustainable Tourism Practices

Eco-Friendly Accommodations
Choose accommodations that prioritize sustainability. Look for hotels and resorts that have eco-certifications, use renewable energy sources, implement water conservation measures, and support local initiatives for environmental protection. Consider

staying in eco-friendly lodges, boutique hotels with green certifications, or eco-conscious Airbnb listings that promote responsible tourism.

Sustainable Transportation
Opt for eco-friendly transportation options to explore Austin. Use public transportation like buses and trains whenever possible. Many areas in Austin are bike-friendly, so consider renting a bike or using bike-sharing services to move around the city sustainably. Walking is also a great way to discover Austin's neighborhoods while reducing carbon emissions.

Support Local and Sustainable Dining
Indulge in Austin's culinary delights while supporting local and sustainable dining practices. Choose restaurants and eateries that source ingredients from local farmers and producers, prioritize organic and seasonal menu items, and implement sustainable food practices such as reducing food waste and promoting recycling. Explore Austin's vibrant food truck scene, where many vendors focus on sustainable and ethical food practices.

Reduce Single-Use Plastic
Austin is committed to reducing single-use plastic waste, and as a responsible traveler, you can contribute to this effort. Carry a reusable water bottle and refill it at water stations throughout the city. Bring a reusable shopping bag for your purchases and avoid single-use plastic bags. Say no to plastic straws and utensils, and opt for eco-friendly alternatives like bamboo or stainless steel options.

Respect Nature and Wildlife

When exploring Austin's outdoor attractions such as parks, trails, and natural reserves, remember to respect nature and wildlife. Stay on designated paths to avoid damaging sensitive ecosystems. Dispose of waste properly in designated bins and follow Leave No Trace principles by taking your trash with you. Observe wildlife from a distance and avoid feeding or disturbing them.

Support Local Arts and Culture

Immerse yourself in Austin's vibrant arts and culture scene while supporting local artists and artisans. Visit galleries, museums, and cultural centers that showcase Austin's rich artistic heritage. Purchase souvenirs and gifts from local artists and craft markets to support the local economy and promote sustainable tourism practices.

Learn About Austin's Sustainability Initiatives

Take the time to learn about Austin's sustainability initiatives and green projects. Attend eco-friendly events, workshops, and seminars to gain insights into environmental conservation efforts in the city. Participate in community clean-up activities or volunteer with local organizations working on sustainability projects to make a positive impact during your visit.

Respect Local Communities

Respect the local communities in Austin by observing cultural norms, traditions, and customs. Be mindful of noise levels, especially in residential areas, and follow local regulations and guidelines. Engage with locals respectfully, learn about their culture, and support community-based tourism initiatives that empower local residents.

Practice Responsible Tourism Photography
Capture memorable moments responsibly by practicing ethical tourism photography. Respect privacy and seek permission before photographing individuals, especially in cultural or religious settings.

Avoid intruding on private property or restricted areas for the sake of photography, and refrain from posting geotagged locations that may impact sensitive natural habitats or communities.

Leave a Positive Impact
Leave a positive impact during your stay in Austin by sharing your experiences and insights with others. Encourage fellow travelers to adopt sustainable tourism practices and support local businesses, conservation efforts, and community initiatives. Leave reviews and feedback that highlight sustainable tourism experiences and inspire others to travel responsibly.

Chapter 15:

Useful Resources

Tourist Information Centers

Austin Visitor Center

Located in the heart of downtown Austin at 602 E. Fourth St., the Austin Visitor Center is your gateway to discovering the city's attractions, events, and hidden gems. Operated by Visit Austin, the official tourism organization for the city, this center provides a wealth of resources for tourists.

Services Offered: The center offers maps, brochures, and guides detailing Austin's top attractions, dining options, outdoor activities, and cultural experiences. Knowledgeable staff members are available to answer questions, provide recommendations, and assist with trip planning.

Events and Tours: Stay updated on upcoming events, festivals, and guided tours through the center's information boards and interactive displays. They can also help you book tours and experiences across Austin and the surrounding Hill Country.

Gift Shop: Don't forget to browse through the gift shop for unique Austin souvenirs, local artwork, and keepsakes to commemorate your trip.

Austin-Bergstrom International Airport Visitor Information Center

For travelers arriving by air, the Austin-Bergstrom International Airport Visitor Information Center offers convenient access to essential resources right upon landing.

Location: You can find the visitor information center in the baggage claim area of the Barbara Jordan Terminal.

Services: Obtain maps, transportation information, and brochures about Austin's attractions, accommodations, and dining options. Friendly staff can assist with airport-related inquiries as well as general tourist information.

Transportation Assistance: Learn about public transportation options, shuttle services, rental cars, and rideshare availability to navigate Austin seamlessly from the airport to your destination.

Regional Tourist Information Centers

In addition to central tourist centers, several regional information centers cater to specific areas of interest around Austin.

Texas Hill Country Visitor Center: Situated west of Austin, this center at 10680 W. State Highway 29 in Dripping Springs provides insights into the Hill Country's wineries, outdoor activities, scenic drives, and historic sites.

San Antonio Visitor Information Centers: If you're planning day trips to San Antonio or exploring nearby attractions, such as the Alamo and River Walk, the visitor information centers in San Antonio offer comprehensive guidance and maps.

Fredericksburg Visitor Information Center: For those venturing into the charming town of Fredericksburg, renowned for its German heritage, wine tastings, and unique shops, stop by the visitor center at 302 E. Austin St. for assistance and local recommendations.

Online Resources and Mobile Apps
In today's digital age, accessing information on-the-go is essential. Take advantage of online resources and mobile apps to enhance your Austin experience.

Visit Austin Website: Visit Austin's official website (https://www.austintexas.org/) is a treasure trove of information, including event calendars, travel guides, hotel bookings, dining directories, and insider tips.

Mobile Apps: Download the Visit Austin mobile app for real-time updates on events, attractions, restaurants, and transportation options. Other helpful apps include public transit apps for bus schedules, rideshare apps for convenient travel, and navigation apps for exploring Austin's neighborhoods.

Local Guides and Brochures
While wandering through Austin's neighborhoods, keep an eye out for local guides and brochures available at hotels, restaurants, and attractions.

Walking Tour Maps: Pick up walking tour maps to explore downtown Austin's historic districts, street art, and architectural landmarks at your own pace.

Event Flyers: Discover live music venues, art galleries, theater performances, and cultural events by checking out event flyers and posters around the city.

Restaurant Guides: Find culinary delights in Austin's diverse food scene with restaurant guides highlighting BBQ joints, food trucks, farm-to-table eateries, and international cuisine.

Emergency and Safety Information
Lastly, ensure you have access to emergency contacts and safety information during your stay in Austin.

Emergency Numbers: Save essential phone numbers, including emergency services (911), local police, fire department, and medical facilities, in case of emergencies.

Safety Tips: Familiarize yourself with safety tips for navigating Austin, such as staying hydrated during hot weather, practicing traffic safety while biking or walking, and being aware of wildlife in outdoor areas.

Online Resources and Apps

Visit Austin Website (https://www.austintexas.org/): The official tourism website of Austin is a treasure trove of information. Here, you can find comprehensive guides on attractions, events, dining options, accommodations, and more. It's a one-stop-shop for planning your Austin adventure.

Austin360 (https://www.austin360.com/): For the latest news, events, and entertainment in Austin, Austin360 is your go-to source. From live music performances to food festivals, this website keeps you updated on everything happening in the city.

Austin Chronicle (https://www.austinchronicle.com/): Dive into Austin's cultural scene with the Austin Chronicle. This publication covers arts, music, food, and local news, offering insights into the city's vibrant culture.

Google Maps and Waze: Navigating Austin's streets can be a breeze with these navigation apps. Google Maps provides detailed directions, transit options, and real-time traffic updates, while Waze offers community-driven traffic and road information.

CapMetro App: Austin's public transportation system, Capital Metro, has its official app. You can plan your bus or train route, check schedules, and even purchase tickets directly from your smartphone.

Yelp and TripAdvisor: When it comes to finding the best restaurants, bars, and attractions in Austin, Yelp and TripAdvisor are invaluable. Read reviews, view photos, and make informed decisions about where to eat and what to do.

OpenTable and Resy: For dining reservations, OpenTable and Resy are popular choices. Whether you're craving Texas barbecue or gourmet cuisine, these apps let you book tables at Austin's top restaurants with ease.

Eventbrite and Ticketmaster: Keep track of upcoming events, concerts, and festivals in Austin with Eventbrite and Ticketmaster. Purchase tickets in advance to secure your spot at popular shows and performances.

Austin Public Library (https://library.austintexas.gov/): Beyond books, the Austin Public Library offers a range of resources for visitors. Access free Wi-Fi, attend cultural programs, and explore their digital collections during your stay.

Austin Weather App: Stay informed about the weather conditions in Austin with a reliable weather app. From sunny days at Barton Springs Pool to occasional rain showers, knowing the forecast helps you plan outdoor activities accordingly.

ParkATX App: Parking in downtown Austin can be challenging, but the ParkATX app makes it easier. Pay for parking, locate available spots, and avoid parking tickets with this convenient tool.

Uber and Lyft: For convenient rides around Austin, Uber and Lyft are popular ride-sharing options. Whether you're heading to a restaurant or exploring nightlife on Sixth Street, these apps offer hassle-free transportation.

Airbnb and Vrbo: If you're looking for unique accommodations beyond hotels, Airbnb and Vrbo have a wide range of options in Austin. From cozy downtown lofts to spacious Hill Country retreats, find the perfect place to stay for your trip.

Local News Apps (KVUE, KXAN, Austin American-Statesman): Stay updated on local news, weather alerts, and events with Austin's news apps. KVUE, KXAN, and the Austin American-Statesman keep you informed about what's happening in the city.

Austin Trails and Parks Apps: Explore Austin's outdoor beauty with apps dedicated to trails and parks. Discover scenic hiking routes, biking trails, and picturesque green spaces across the city.

Conclusion and Final Tips:

Farewell and Safe Travels

As you prepare to bid farewell to Austin, Texas, after an unforgettable journey filled with vibrant culture, rich history, and mesmerizing experiences, here are some final tips and insights to ensure your departure is as smooth as your time spent in this remarkable city.

Departure Preparation Before leaving Austin, double-check your travel documents, including passports, visas, and any necessary permits. Ensure you have copies of important documents stored securely, both physically and digitally. Confirm your transportation arrangements to the airport or your next destination, whether it's by car, shuttle service, or public transport.

Gratitude and Feedback Express your gratitude to the locals who made your stay memorable, from hotel staff to tour guides and restaurant servers. Leave positive feedback and reviews for businesses and attractions you enjoyed; your words can inspire others to explore Austin and contribute to the local economy. Consider sharing your experiences on social media to spread the word about this dynamic city.

Responsible Tourism Continue practicing responsible tourism by respecting local customs, traditions, and the environment. Dispose of waste properly, recycle where possible, and support eco-friendly initiatives. Consider offsetting your travel carbon footprint through reputable organizations dedicated to environmental conservation.

Memories and Souvenirs Capture your favorite moments in Austin through photographs, journals, or souvenirs that hold sentimental value. Whether it's a handmade craft from a local artisan or a postcard depicting Austin's iconic skyline, these mementos will serve as lasting reminders of your time in the city.

Stay Connected Stay connected with Austin even after you leave by following local news, events, and cultural happenings online. Join travel forums or social media groups dedicated to Austin to stay updated on recommendations from fellow travelers and residents. Consider planning a return trip to explore more of what Austin has to offer.

Safety Reminders As with any travel, prioritize your safety by remaining aware of your surroundings, especially in crowded areas or unfamiliar neighborhoods. Keep emergency contacts handy, including local police, hospitals, and your country's embassy or consulate. Travel insurance can provide additional peace of mind in case of unforeseen events.

Farewell to Austin As you board your flight or embark on your next adventure, take a moment to reflect on the diverse experiences Austin has gifted you. From live music and outdoor adventures to culinary delights and cultural discoveries, Austin leaves a lasting impression on all who visit. Carry the spirit of

Austin with you wherever you go, and may your travels be filled with joy, discovery, and meaningful connections.

Safe travels, and until we meet again in the vibrant streets of Austin, Texas!

Made in United States
North Haven, CT
07 November 2024

59990995R00124